The HIDDEN HISTORY *of* SOUTHEAST TENNESSEE

The HIDDEN HISTORY *of* SOUTHEAST TENNESSEE

JOE GUY

THE History PRESS

Published by The History Press
Charleston, SC 29403
www.historypress.net

First published 2011

Manufactured in the United States

ISBN 978.1.59629.855.2

Guy, Joe D.
The hidden history of southeast Tennessee / Joe Guy.
p. cm.
ISBN 978-1-59629-855-2
1. Tennessee--History--Anecdotes. 2. Tennessee, East--History--Anecdotes. 3. Tennessee--Social life and customs--Anecdotes. 4. Tennessee--Biography--Anecdotes. 5. Tennessee--History, Local--Anecdotes. I. Title.
F436.6.G89 2010
976.8--dc22
2010019035

Notice: The information in this book is true and complete to the best of our knowledge. It is offered without guarantee on the part of the author or The History Press. The author and The History Press disclaim all liability in connection with the use of this book.

For my fourth great-grandfather, William Morgan, who does not appear in this book but is quietly intertwined within its stories. Grandfather William lies beneath the clay at Big Creek Cemetery in Monroe County, and he whispers his wisdom to me through the 180-year-old inscription carved meticulously on his gravestone.

Yes, Grandfather, some day I will be like you…

Contents

Introduction 9

Part I. Stories from East Tennessee

The Good Boat *Adventure* 11

Spencer Jarnagin: McMinn County's Lost Senator 14

The Governor's Bible 16

The Lost Settlement of Polk County 20

Hiking through the Old Dutch Settlement 22

Looking for De Soto's Trail 27

Part II. Indians

The Old Soldier, Friend of the Cherokee 31

Cherokees in Charles Town, 1759 34

Wilderness Survival in Eighteenth-century Tennessee: The James Smith Story 37

The Assassination of Jack Walker 41

The Overbearing Governor 43

Part III. The Civil War

"They Killed Him at Goodsprings" 47

Where the Travelers Rested 50

Uncle Pat 52

"The Yanks Have Fortified the Courthouse" 54

The Price of War: The Van Dyke Sons 57
Daphney's Thanksgiving 60
Forrest's Battle at Calhoun 63

Part IV. Ghosts, Graves and Other Strange Happenings
A Mausoleum, a Legend, a School and Angelina 67
Old Steel, Cradles and Graves 71
The Grave Robbers 73
Haunted Williamsburg 75
Dead Man's Ticket 77
Houses of the Dead 79
The Dead and the Almost Dead 82

Part V. Politics, Small Towns and Giant People
Etowah's Doughboys 85
One Street Corner, a Thousand Stories 88
"Going to the Store" in Early Etowah 90
The Athens Academy 92
Indians, Senators and Governors: The Forest Hill Academy 94
The Underdogs: Cook High's 1933 Basketball Team 97
Miss Myrtle 99
The Campbell–Van Dyke Graves 102

Part VI. Holidays and Traditions
George Burger's Christmas 105
No Fake Christmas Trees, Beagles and Mamaw's House 108
Cat Heads for Breakfast 110

About the Author 112

Introduction

Once again, there are stories to tell.

During the course of researching the stories for this book, Stephanie and I have traveled over much of Southeast Tennessee in order to bring you more of the lesser-known history of this fascinating region that I call home. We've been to cemeteries and lone graves, sites of murders, ghostly old houses and down many a country road to obtain documentation and photographs. A few times, we even took the boys, and the boys took their new iPods.

This is the third such compilation of stories that my family and I have worked together to publish. They don't get much credit for all the things that I get to do, but they are always there, riding along, keeping me company, trekking through the woods and even listening as I recant some tale from the distant past. Sometimes, they even show interest and might even really believe that ol' dad actually knows what he is talking about.

These stories are a part of all of us who live in Southeast Tennessee, and I hope you enjoy them. I know that when I research and write these stories, I feel a real attachment to the people and places that the stories are about. Where legends are recalled, I try to make note. Otherwise, all of the stories in this book are true and are part of the history of this corner of our state. The stories are as rich as the soil that covers the graves and paths of those who walked here before us and who left these fantastic characters and tales that are hidden in our past.

Part I
Stories from East Tennessee

For the stories in this first part, I visited libraries, hiked into a lost mountain settlement and held a governor's Bible. The stories hidden in Southeast Tennessee's history are varied and many, so let's begin with an "adventure."

The Good Boat *Adventure*

On December 22, 1779, a flatboat pushed off from the Long Island of the Holston in present-day Kingsport. The name of the boat was *Adventure*, and on board were Colonel John Donelson and his family. Donelson kept a diary to record the trip, which today is a valued piece of Tennessee history. His twelve-year-old daughter Rachael, who accompanied him, would also be notable for another reason: she later became Mrs. Andrew Jackson.

The *Adventure* and a flotilla of some thirty smaller boats, all carrying a total of about two hundred people, drifted down the Tennessee River. The intention was to navigate the Tennessee to the mouth of the Cumberland and then go up the Cumberland to Big Salt Lick, where the people hoped to settle. Another group of settlers was traveling overland, driving livestock. Among these men taking the land route were James Robertson and Ephraim Peyton.

The boats made it as far as the mouth of Reedy's Creek, but the river became too icy. After almost two months of waiting for the ice to melt, they made it as far as Cloud's Creek on February 20, where they spent a week. On the twenty-seventh, they had not gone far when the *Adventure*, along with the boats of Mr. Boyd and Mr. Rounsever, struck a shoal and became stuck until the following night, when the waters rose enough for the boats to break free. For the next week or so, the boats bumped their way along, passing the mouth of the French Broad (just north of present Knoxville) on March 2; on this day, Hugh Henry's boat struck an island and sank. The other boats were put to shore, and men were able to raise Henry's boat and repair it, although another problem was found: young Reuben Harrison had gone hunting and had not returned. For two days they waited, but fearing that he'd been killed by Indians, the boats regretfully set off again on March 4, leaving behind old Mr. Harrison and a few others who wished to continue the search. Fortunately, Rueben was found farther downriver that morning, having appeared only to have lost his way. At about 3:00 p.m., the *Adventure* passed the mouth of the Little Tennessee (present Lenoir City). The flotilla passed the mouth of the Clinch (present Kingston) on the fifth.

On March 7, winds made the water dangerous for the smaller craft, and the entire flotilla went to shore, with passengers camping in a deserted Indian village. On this day, a child was born to Mrs. Ephraim Peyton.

The next day, the boats came upon several Chickamauga Indian villages (just north of Chattanooga) that were heavily populated. Some of the Indians tried to wave to boats close to their shore, while others came out in canoes and wearing war paint. A half-breed, Archy Coody, came on board the *Adventure* and told Donelson to drift past these towns. He stayed with the *Adventure* for about an hour and, upon leaving, declared that all dangerous villages had been passed. But the next day, another village was encountered (near present Moccasin Bend), and when one of the boats drifted too close, shots rang out, killing a man named Payne on John Blackmore's boat. The last boat in the fleet was that of the Stewart family, who were bringing up the rear due to them having contracted smallpox. The Indians were able to cut off the Stewarts and either killed or made prisoners of the entire crew.

The *Adventure* then entered the narrows, where the river passes through the Cumberland Mountains. It was hoped that this portion of the journey would be safe, but the Indians continued to pursue and fired upon the flotilla from the cliffs above the river. During one of these episodes, with all of the men busy firing back, Jenny Gower took the helm of her father's boat and steered it through a hazardous part of the river, all while being shot at by the Indians. Later, her clothing was found to be pierced several times with

The Tennessee River in March 2010, as it curves through East Tennessee. The *Adventure*, Colonel John Donelson's flatboat, passed through here in March 1780 on its way south, along with a flotilla of other settlers. The *Adventure* was soon to encounter the violence of the Chickamauga Cherokees. *Photo by Stephanie Guy.*

musket balls, but her only wound was a slight cut to her thigh. Unfortunately, the Jenningses' boat was caught on a rock, and the Jennings family was cut off from the rest of the group. On board was Mrs. Peyton, who was Mr. Jennings's daughter.

The following day, the others were happy to see Mr. Jennings floating up behind them, but he told a sad tale: he had fought hard with the Indians, throwing everything possible overboard to lighten the boat and free it from the rock. He had succeeded, but in the confusion, Mrs. Peyton had somehow thrown her newborn overboard.

The party passed Muscle Shoals on March 12. The passengers were fired upon or threatened by Indians several times over the next few days. Once, the entire party evacuated a camp but left a black man sleeping by the fire. The next day, John Donelson Jr. took a canoe, returned to the camp and found the man still asleep. He returned with Donelson to the others. On March 24, they began the difficult journey up the Cumberland River.

Finally, after a freezing winter navigating dangerous shoals, enduring weather and cold and fighting and eluding Indians, the *Adventure* reached the Big Salt Lick on April 24, 1780. The flotilla found Robertson and the overland party already there, and of course there was much celebration. The Donelsons and many of the other people were among the first of what was known as the Cumberland Settlements, centered on Fort Nashborough (later Nashville). This was one of many such parties that would either come by land or river to expand the settlement of Tennessee, but thanks to Donelson's journal, this is the most famous. The *Adventure* had been aptly named.

SPENCER JARNAGIN: MCMINN COUNTY'S LOST SENATOR

Spencer Jarnagin rises like a ghost from pages of old newspapers and other historical documents—brief glimpses of a man who has eluded the research efforts of both myself and local attorney Bill Buckley. Over the past few years, Bill and I have been able to piece together the life of this man, each sharing the little pieces of information that we have stumbled across. But finally we've discovered this "lost senator" and the story behind him.

Spencer Jarnagin was born in Richland Creek in Grainger County, Tennessee, in 1792 (some sources say April or September 17, 1794), the son of Chelsey and Martha Barton Jarnagin. Spencer pursued classical studies and graduated from Greenville College in 1813. Then he studied law under Judge Hugh Lawson White, was admitted to the bar in 1817 and commenced a practice in Knoxville. He served as a state senator from 1833 to 1835.

In 1835–36, he represented Tom (James) Foreman and Addison Springston in the John Walker murder trial. Foreman and Springston were two Cherokee half brothers accused of the murder of Chief John Walker Jr., which had occurred in McMinn County (today the location is in Bradley County on Benton Pike) in August 1834. The outcome of this trial, and Jarnagin's defense strategy, was a contributing factor in the Cherokee Removal of 1836–38.

Jarnagin presented the defense that the Tennessee court had no legal basis to hear the case, as the Cherokees could not be tried in a state court for a crime that occurred on Cherokee soil. Judge Charles F. Keith agreed and dismissed the trial on this plea, but the decision was overturned by the Tennessee Supreme Court in July 1835 (see the *Chattanooga Times*, June 28,

1836, and Attorney General George S. Yerger's *Yerger's Reports*, vol. 8, *Cases Argued and Determined in the Supreme Court of Tennessee, Knoxville*, July term, 1835). This court decision would eventually be cited as case law to show that the Cherokee Nation was subject to the state courts, and this led to the revocation of Cherokee rights, which allowed for their removal in 1838.

After the trial, Jarnagin moved to Athens in 1837, and it was here where he married Mary Ann Kinder on June 20. He practiced law and was a trustee on the board of directors of the original Forest Hill Academy, as well as a trustee of East Tennessee College (now University of Tennessee) from 1836 to 1851. According to contemporary newspaper accounts, Jarnagin lived near the academy "in the vicinity of the Big Spring in Athens" (*Athens Post*, October, 18, 1849), and his residence was called "Oak Grove House, west end of Athens" (*Athens Post*, January 23, 1852). This would have been in the area of the present E.G. Fisher Library. Jarnagin was a presidential elector on the Whig ticket in 1840 and a Whig nominee for United States senator in 1841, but the General Assembly adjourned without electing a senator. He was later appointed as a Whig to the United States Senate and served from October 17, 1843, to March 3, 1847, as well as served as chairman on the Committee on Revolutionary Claims (documents from the Twenty-eighth Congress can be located at the Library of Congress).

It was during this time that Bill says that Jarnagin found himself in a political mess. In the wake of President Polk's efforts to pass a lower tariff (known as the "Walker Tariff"), special attention was placed on Jarnagin. Although a fellow Tennessean, and having been pressured to support the president's tariff, he was a bitter political enemy of Polk's. What was surprising was that Jarnagin overcame his personal opposition to the president, as well as to the tariff, and actually cast the deciding vote that allowed the tariff to pass. Jarnagin's wisdom seems justified, as Bill says that "despite the fears of its opponents, the Walker Tariff of 1846 resulted in neither the ruin of the manufacturing nor the agricultural sectors of our economy. Instead, it produced a great stream of revenue into the coffers of the United States economy and helped to stabilize the country soon to be torn asunder by a great and internal civil strife."

In the fall of 1849, the Jarnagins mourned the tragic death of their infant daughter, Mary. Perhaps this is what caused the family to leave Athens and move to Memphis, where Spencer continued to practice law. He was an unsuccessful candidate for reelection to the Senate but, for several years, was a member of the Tennessee Supreme Court. Of Judge Jarnagin's legal career, it was said that "he was a brilliant and effective speaker, possessing

Two of Spencer Jarnagin's children, David and Mary, lie in Cedar Grove Cemetery in Athens. Little Mary's death in 1852 could have been a motivating factor for Spencer to move the family across the state to the new town of Memphis. *Photo by Stephanie Guy.*

a mind of quickness and energy, and an imagination of exceeding fertility. He had great powers of ridicule, and when opportunity afforded, could use invective with crushing effect." He died in Memphis on June 25, 1853, and was buried there at Elmwood Cemetery. His wife, Mary, died in Chattanooga on March 25, 1883.

Another interesting local connection is that of the McCallie School in Chattanooga. One of Spencer's daughters, Ellen, married Thomas McCallie in Cleveland in 1862. In 1905, two of their sons—Spencer Jarnagin McCallie and Dr. James Park McCallie—founded the McCallie School in Chattanooga on land donated to them for that purpose by their father.

The Governor's Bible

Not long ago, an artifact was loaned to me that was probably one of the most interesting relics of state and local history that I had ever seen: the Governor Joseph McMinn Bible.

Born in 1758 in West Chester County, Pennsylvania, little is known of Joseph McMinn as a young man. He married Hannah Cooper in 1785 and, the following year, made his way to Hancock County in what would later be the state of Tennessee. In 1790, he was appointed to a county office by territorial governor William Blount, allowing McMinn to enter politics. He became a member of the territorial legislature in 1794 and was part of the state constitutional convention in 1796, actually carrying a copy of the state constitution to Secretary of State Timothy Pickering in Philadelphia. He later served three terms as Speaker of the Tennessee Senate from 1805 to 1809.

After Hannah died in 1811, McMinn next married Miss Rebecca Kincaid, but the marriage only lasted until 1815, when Rebecca died. This was also the year when McMinn was first elected governor. He served three terms, from 1815 to 1821, with his administration handling several Indian treaties and land cessions. While governor, he married Nancy Williams at Fort Southwest Point (now Kingston) in 1818. After serving as governor, he was appointed agent to the Cherokee Indians in 1823. While serving in this capacity, he died at his desk in Calhoun, Tennessee, in 1824 and is buried there. McMinn County bears Joseph McMinn's name chiefly because the Hiwassee Purchase, out of which the county was formed, took place during his governorship.

To actually have the governor's Bible to study was a real pleasure. First of all, few people knew it even existed. It is now in the possession of a family in Bradley County, who were kind enough to loan it to me to photograph, transcribe and study. The Bible is large and leather bound. Inside the front cover is posted "Joseph McMinn." Except for the missing back cover, the Bible is almost entirely whole and in relatively good shape for its age. A few pages over, near the front, is written "Joseph McMinn Bible Bought of David Wendle January 1819 Rec'd $16.00." This is probably a receipt from when McMinn purchased the Bible during his governorship; $16 was a high price in those days, equal to about $261 today.

The "Family Information" pages are reproduced below. Some of this information, to my knowledge, has never before been made available to the public. The original text is below, unless otherwise indicated with notes in brackets:

Family Record; Births, Deaths

First [Marriage]
Joseph McMinn son of Robert and Sarah McMinn was born 22 June 1758, near West Chester Pennsylvania, and married to his wife Hannah Cooper on the 9th day of May 1785, she being the daughter of James and Rosanna Cooper, and was born 20th June 1760, in Chester County Pennsylvania near Piqua Church

Second Marriage
Joseph McMinn was married to his wife Rebecca Kincaid on the 5th January 1812, she was born in Carter's Valley Hawkins County State of Tennessee, on the 7th October 1793 and was the daughter of David and Mary Kincaid

Third Marriage
Joseph McMinn was married to his wife Nancy Williams at Southwest Point, Roane County & State of Tennessee on the 4th August 1816, she being the daughter of James and Phenobe Glasgow, and was born in Green County State of North Carolina in the 22 day of April 1770

Hetty McMinn daughter of John and Mary McMinn was married to Robert Morrison both of Hawkins County and State of Tennessee on the 11th day of May 1823.

Jane McMinn daughter of Joseph and Hannah McMinn was born on 27th August 1787 at one o'clock AM in Hawkins County now State of Tennessee. And died on 28 January 1815 at her own residence in Hawkins County aforesaid.

The aforesaid Jane was married to Hugh Campbell esquire merchant Rogersville on the 9th day of May 1804 in Hawkins County aforesaid Who died 27th Sept 1804 in Rogersville aforesaid of a cholera-morbus, and something like the yellow fever

Jane Campbell relict of Hugh aforesaid was married to Major James P. Goins in the 20th November 1808 in neither of those marriages has she any issue

Eldrige H. Morrison son of Robert & Hetty Morrison was born 25 day of September 1831

Sarah Ann Morrison daughter of Robert and Hetty Morrison was born 17 November 1833

Hetty McMinn Daughter of John and Mary McMinn was born 13th May 1801 in Hawkins County, and on the death of her mother, was adopted into my family, and was in all respects attended to as one of its numbers.

Mary p. Morrison, daughter of Robert and Hetty Morrison was born 2n Day of September 1829

Joseph L. Morrison son of Rbt and Hetty Morrisson was born 2 Jan 1824

George W. Morrison
Son of Robt and Hetty Morrison was born 4 January 1826

William H. Morrison
Son of Robert and Hetty Morrison was born 29 of September 1824

Hannah McMinn wife of said Joseph McMinn Died on the 27th of February 1811 of an inward inflammation, which terminated her life in 5 days illness, aged 49 years 8 month & 7 days and departed at her own dwelling in Hawkins County Ten.

Joseph McMinn Died
October 17 1824

[continuing notes appear to be left by McMinn's descendants]

Marthy Ann Morrison daughter of Robert and Hetty Morrison was born the 31 of August 1843

Robert Morrison son of Thomas and Jane Morrison was born January the 7 1796

Rebecca McMinn wife of Joseph McMinn died on the 11th January 1815 of a nervous fever of 29 days continuous. Aged twenty one years & nine months.

Jane Goines [Gaines?] *wife of James T. Goins & daughter of Joseph and Hannah McMinn died on the 27 January 1815 of what was called the cold plague or epidemic, in an illness of something less than three days, from a perfect state of good health, aged twenty seven years and 9 months.*

Sarah Ann Morrison Daughter of Robert & Hetty Morrison died on the 3 November in the year 1836 died with the mesels & whooping cough age 2 years and 10 months

Martha Morrison imbraced religion 1856 [written in pencil]

George Morrison son of Robert & Hetty Morrison died on the 2ont of February about 4 o'clock in the PM in the year of our lord one thousand eight hundred and forty two aged 16 years and twenty eight days.

Robert Morrison husband of Hetty Morrison died the 19th day of April AD 1854 of flux aged 58 years 4 months

Here ends the transcription. No other handwritten notations were found in the Bible.

The Lost Settlement of Polk County

After the Cherokee Removal in 1837–38, a gentleman from New York City named Christian Dietzsh traveled to the newly opened lands in Southeast Tennessee and obtained land along Big Creek in the Ocoee District, on the south side of the Ocoee River and near Big Frog Mountain in Polk County, Tennessee. Dietzsh built a road into his land and tried to make a living of it, but after a while he gave up and returned to New York. He told an acquaintance in the city about his lands in Tennessee, a man named Edward Bayer.

Bayer was a wealthy Brooklyn banker, and seeing an opportunity to purchase a lot of cheap land, he bought more than 200,000 acres in Monroe, McMinn and Polk Counties. Bayer's wife, Adele, and her younger sister, Rosine Parmentier, were actively involved in promoting social improvements in New York, and with Edward's land purchase in East Tennessee, they saw an opportunity to direct immigrants to a remote community that would be isolated from many of the social ills that plagued the larger cities. In 1847, they began to recruit immigrant families, especially those skilled in a trade, to move to the East Tennessee mountain land that Edward owned. Several German, Italian and French families—with names such as Linder, Weber, Miolani, Guerrin, Muller, Nochoriner, Gianelli and Beckler—made the long trip and took up residence on a tributary of Sylco Creek, which came to be known as Dutch Creek.

The settlers entered what was, for the most part, an untamed wilderness. But they were undaunted and took to building homes, mills (with dams and races) and forges, clearing land for fields and planting orchards and vineyards. So many vineyards were planted that the place was known by some as "Vineland." The community grew, and before long fine wines and expertly crafted furniture were being produced there. They were almost entirely self-supporting and had such little contact with the other residents of Polk County that they referred to anyone outside the settlement as "Americans."

In 1852, curious as to the success of their mountain community, Edward and Adele, along with Rosine, visited the remote region to take a firsthand look at their tenants. Rosine kept a journal of the trip, which today is a valuable historical record that provides a brief look into the settlement and its people.

The trip began on October 2 with a three-day journey on a steamship from New York to Savannah. From Savannah, they took the Central Railroad to Macon, went north on the Western and Atlantic to Atlanta and on to Dalton and then went on the East Tennessee and Georgia Railroad to Cleveland. From Cleveland they took wagons eastward, along the rough "Copper Road" that led toward the mines in the Copper Basin. Just above the site of the present Parksville Dam, the party crossed the river toward Sylco Creek. After crossing the creek almost thirty times and getting lost in the dark, they finally came upon the house of Napoleon Guerin, the settlement's manager, at about ten o'clock at night on Friday, October 8.

Rosine's journal speaks of the many visits they made with the Gianellis, Miolanis, Linders and others, as well as Mr. Chable, who was employed by Edward Bayer as a civil engineer. She wrote of the settlers that "these people have shown a great deal of industry and perseverance, for they had absolutely nothing when they commenced and now their fields and everything about them are in good order." She noticed that the people were so healthy and that "everybody seems to grow younger in this country." She mentioned that the Gianelli house was hardly visible for the grapevines that grew around it. On another day, Rosine, Edward and Adele followed Mr. Gerrin on a hike to the top of Big Frog Mountain. They hiked to several other locations during their visit and enjoyed picnics beside the mountain springs. She noted that the settlement would benefit from a new post office that had recently been established at Sylco, some five miles away. After several days of visits and observation, the Bayers and Rosine left the settlement on Saturday, October 30, and returned to New York over the route on which they had come.

For many more years, the settlement continued. But as its children grew and sought husbands and wives from the surrounding "Americans," the community began to dissimilate. By the late 1800s, only the Becklers remained. The fine houses and mills eventually withered away, and by the time the land was taken over by the U.S. Forest Service in the 1930s, only a few crumbling buildings still stood. Today the area is much like the wilderness it was when the first settlers came—overgrown and remote, the dwelling place of deer, boar and rattlesnake.

In the fall, though, if you know how to find the old road, a hiker can still explore the area. The remains of roads, foundations and springs are still there, hidden by overgrowth and a century's worth of autumn leaves that cover the last remnants of a great social experiment. It is a lost place, but it remains in the legends and histories of local families who are descended from the original people of the Old Dutch Settlement.

HIKING THROUGH THE OLD DUTCH SETTLEMENT

I was first introduced to the Old Dutch Settlement in Polk County in 1988. I took a class at Cleveland State under the late Catherine Trewitt, former Bradley County educator and historian/folklorist. That class was one of the most interesting I ever took, and I regret that Mrs. Trewitt never knew the impact that she had on me then that continues today in the writing and research I do.

For a long time, I had wanted to visit the Dutch Settlement site and had been approached about doing a history tour similar to those I often do to the White Cliff/Panther Cave sites on Starr Mountain. But the Dutch Settlement site is much larger and very remote, and without proper knowledge it would be easy to get lost or to entirely miss the sites that still exist there.

Eventually, I was fortunate to work out a hike into the settlement with Mitchell Guinn. Mitchell had been into the area before and had noted GPS coordinates for some of the site locations. He shared my interest in local history, and I was not about to miss the opportunity. My wife, Stephanie, and I met him on a bright Saturday May morning at Cherokee Corners on Highway 64, and we were off.

Again, the site itself is remote and a little hard to reach. There were several miles of winding mountain roads until we parked at Pace Gap and descended down into the eastern end of the settlement site, armed with Mitchell's GPS, Stephanie's camera and my copy of Thurman Parish's *The Old Homeplace*, which is perhaps the best contemporary guide to the location and its history.

The Bachle, or Beckler, family were the longest-dwelling residents of the Old Dutch Settlement—residing in a house on this spot built in 1847—until the last Beckler left in 1927. The author is pictured with Mitchell Guinn, inspecting the remains of the house's foundation and chimneys. *Photo by Stephanie Guy.*

The Saturday was beautiful and sunny, and the old road built by Christian Dietzsh in 1842 (improved by Napoleon Guerin after his arrival in 1847) was still easy to follow, having been somewhat maintained by the forest service. After a few hundred yards, we came into a narrow valley that seemed to literally be crisscrossed with small streams and springs that fed into Dutch Creek, the main water source of the settlement. It was easy to see why the settlement was established and had thrived along the wide, rich bottomland fed by so much water.

We first located what seemed to be some remains of a house site, believed to be that of the Nochorini family. It consisted of two large depressions in a level place just above the road. The Nochorinis were likely Italian and are believed to have been some of the original settlers sent to the area by Edward Bayer in 1847.

We walked farther westward, and the valley opened up into a wide meadow that was the center of the settlement. I imagined that this area must surely have been used to grow the grapes for the wine for which the settlement became known. Several house sites are recorded to have been located in and around this meadow, but we were only able to visit one. On the southern end are the remains of the Beckler field and homesite. This field is maintained by the U.S. Forest Service and Tennessee Wildlife Resource Agency for a wildlife food plot, and it brings to mind what the farmland looked like almost 160 years ago.

The Beckler site is now just a large pile of stones, the only remains of the house built by the family about 1847. The Becklers were German (the name was originally spelled "Bachle"). They were the longest Dutch Settlement residents and were the last to leave in 1927. As we inspected the site, we found that we were not the only visitors: a leg-long blacksnake was sunning itself among the old chimney stones, perhaps a descendant of the ones young Rosine Parmentier mentions in her diary during her visit to the settlement in 1852. Respecting his right to the property, we left him alone. The Weber and Linder homesites were located just to the south, but the blacksnake's cousins might have been enjoying those sites as well, so we took some pictures and GPS readings and continued on down the old road.

This road was the main thoroughfare that connected the settlement. It generally follows Dutch Creek and, in many places, crosses into the creek itself. The settlers would have traveled this road daily to visit, trade and worship together. *Photo by Stephanie Guy.*

The Napoleon Guerin house site. Rosine Parmentier stayed here in 1852 and described the house in great detail. Nonnative decorative plants still grow here, descended from those planted by the Guerin family. *Photo by Stephanie Guy.*

The road passed by and literally through Dutch Creek, which was flowing clear and cold, reflecting the midday spring sun. We thought of the many times the settlers must have traveled it, barefoot or on horseback or wagons, to visit or trade with one another. At some point, we passed the site of the mill but did not investigate to see any remains. Soon we entered another wide meadow, which was the entrance to the settlement. Here at one time stood a blockhouse to guard the entrance, as well as some houses for new settlers in which they could reside until a home was built, and just to the south was the home of the settlement manager, Napoleon Guerin.

Of all the sites, this one was the most special to me. When Rosine Parmentier visited the settlement, she stayed with Mr. Guerin. She described his house as being

> *built on a little hill which slopes toward the west. His garden, which must be beautiful during the summer, is arranged in terraces…His house is wide but only one story high and has a balcony or stoop across the whole*

Part of the stone wall at Guerin's spring, which Rosine described in her diary. Rosine enjoyed the water here, as did the author on this visit. *Photo by Stephanie Guy.*

> *front which makes it very pleasant, for the sun only comes there late in the afternoon. The dining room is in the middle, on the right side is Mr. Guerin's bedroom which serves us as a parlor, and on the left were two small bedrooms which we occupied.*

Today, only two piles of chimney stones remain, with stones from the foundation scattered about. An aged black walnut tree guards the site, along with yucca plants that are possibly from those placed by Guerin himself. We also located Guerin's spring, its rock-lined wall still mostly intact. Rosine drank from this very same water source and also described it in her diary.

Our exploration ended as the afternoon drew to a close, and we hiked out, with plans to return at the next opportunity. Ascending the road out of the settlement, we left behind the silent traces of a long-lost community, of homes and families, of meals cooked in fireplaces, of meal ground by a neighbor and of a young New York girl experiencing her one and only visit to the mountains of East Tennessee and learning the ways of its blacksnakes and the fresh taste of its spring water.

Looking for De Soto's Trail

The name Hernando de Soto is forever tied to the southeastern United States, linked to the Spanish explorer's wandering journey through the region in 1540. Since De Soto made no maps and his travels are only represented in journals kept by some of his men, his actual journey is difficult to pin down and has kept historians scratching their heads for more than 450 years.

The most reliable journal was kept by Rodrigo Rangel, who was De Soto's personal secretary and who traveled along with him. Rangel recorded vivid descriptions of rivers and topography, as well as Native American place names, that today can somewhat be pieced together to form a fair assumption of De Soto's route. Again, without accurate maps, these are only assumptions based on circumstantial evidence. Rangel's writings also give us clues to the question of whether De Soto passed through Southeast Tennessee.

When De Soto embarked on his journey from Charlotte Harbor in Florida on June 1, 1539, he was a wealthy thirty-nine-year-old Spanish nobleman intent on colonizing North America, finding gold and establishing a route to the "northern ocean" he had heard about. With him were soldiers, traders, laborers and clergymen, as well as a few women, all of whom he had recruited in Spain. They brought clothing, armor, guns, powder, horses, pigs, mules and dogs. Throughout the fall of 1539 and spring of 1540, the group traveled northeast through Georgia, South Carolina and North Carolina before turning east into Tennessee. Portions of Rangel's journal indicate the path they took:

> *Monday, which was the last day of May, the Governor* [De Soto] *left from Guasili and went with his army to an oak grove alongside a river, and the next day they passed through Canasoga* [Waynesville, North Carolina] *and spent the night in the open. And on Wednesday they spent the night alongside a swamp…The next day, Thursday, they went alongside a large creek next to the river* [mouth of Tuckasegee River at the Little Tennessee River, five miles east of Bryson City, North Carolina] *that they had crossed in the savannah where the cacica went away, and now it was large. The next day, Friday, they went to a pine forest and a creek, where Indians from Chiaha came in peace and brought corn…Saturday, the fifth of June, was the day that they entered in Chiaha (on an island in the Little Tennessee); and since from Xuala all their travel had been through a mountain range and the horses were tired and thin, and the Christians likewise fatigued.*

If, as it appears, De Soto followed the Little Tennessee River, then his army came into Monroe County:

> *On Monday, the twenty-eighth of June, the Governor and his people left from Chiaha, and they passed through five or six towns, and they went to sleep at a pine forest, but they had much hardship there in crossing a river that flowed very strongly…The next day, Tuesday, they passed through a town* [Cherokee towns of Chota/Tanasi, on the Little Tennessee], *and there they took corn and went onward to sleep in the open. The following Wednesday they crossed a river* [Toqua Creek], *and then a town and the river another time* [likely the Cherokee town of Tuskeegee and the Tellico River where it flows into the Little Tennessee near Vonore], *and they spent the night in the open. And on Thursday the cacique* [chief] *of Coste came forth to receive them in peace, and he led the Christians to sleep in a town of his* [in the area of Athens, Madisonville or Englewood]. *And thus, the next day, Thursday, going toward his principal town of Coste, he slipped away and evaded the Spaniards and called his people to arms. On Friday* [note that Thursday was listed twice above, a common Rangel error; this day, Friday, should be Saturday], *the second day of the month of July, the adelantado Governor* [in advance] *arrived at Coste* [Hiwassee Island in Meigs County], *which is a town on an island of the river, which there flows great and strong and is difficult to enter: and the Christians crossed the first branch without danger to any one of the soldiers.*

If we take Rangel's words as they appear, and assuming that he was being led by the Indians over the paths we know they used, then it is entirely possible that De Soto either traveled through Madisonville and east of Englewood on the Great Indian Warpath before taking the west fork along the Hiwassee River toward Coste or came from Madisonville to Athens on that fork of the Warpath and then to the river at Calhoun, where he turned west toward Coste. Rangel mentions the chief of Coste "leading the Christians to sleep in a town of his." This town would have been somewhere midway between Vonore and Hiwassee Island and was not on any river. It is possible that this "town" may have been the hunting camp that came to be known as Pumpkintown just north of Athens. At this time of year, June/July, the Indians would have been hunting, and

This island at the confluence of the Hiwassee and Tennessee Rivers is believed to have held ancient Native American settlements for twelve thousand years. Evidence strongly suggests that this is the town of Coste mentioned in the journals kept by De Soto's secretary—the Spanish explorers visited it on July 2, 1540. Today, much of the island, viewed here from the bluffs across the river, is under the waters of Chickamauga Lake. *Photo by Stephanie Guy.*

Pumpkintown could have been occupied with temporary houses, so Rangel would have thought that it was a town.

Again, this is only speculation, but the possibility is certainly there. We will never know the exact route De Soto followed, nor exactly where he camped—only that he was in the area. But he could have camped at Pumpkintown before going on south.

Of course, De Soto eventually wandered to the Mississippi, where he died and was buried in the river that he discovered, never finding the gold or the trade routes he desired. But he left his imprint in the memories of the Indians he encountered, as well as in the vague accounts of his men, forming a mixture of facts, legends and mystery about where he passed.

Part II
Indians

Few aspects of East Tennessee history bring so much attention as our Cherokee Indian heritage. From the stone artifacts that still turn up in farm fields to creek and river names, the presence of the Cherokees is still felt here. Stories of the Indians remain, even after 180 years, and remind us of the proud and noble people who came before us, as well as the less-than-noble whites who changed the Cherokees' lives forever.

The Old Soldier, Friend of the Cherokee

The worried clerk entered the colonel's office at the Cherokee Agency, not really wanting to make the request he was about to make. The request was not in any way difficult; what concerned him the most was the fact that he knew what the old soldier's answer would be. "The Indian is going to stay," said the clerk, "but his family is concerned about sleeping outside on a winter night." The old man looked up from his papers and smiled. "Now, that would not be proper for our guest," he said. "Tell him he may sleep in my own room, in my own bed. I will use one of the tents and sleep in the yard." The clerk nodded and stepped back outside to inform the Indian. He shook his head at the colonel's hospitality and thought, "This will be the death of him."

Weeks later, after having grown sicker from the night in the January air, and already weak with age, Colonel Return Jonathan Meigs died at eighty-three years of age on January 23, 1823, and was buried at the Agency Cemetery along the banks of the Tennessee River, ending a life that few other men could ever dream of living.

Return J. Meigs was born in 1740 in Middletown, Connecticut. He served in the local militia and, by 1774, was a captain. As the Revolutionary War began to unfold, he led a company of light infantry to Boston in April 1775 and was assigned the rank of major in the Continental army. Later that year, he accompanied Colonel Benedict Arnold on his expedition to Canada; he was captured by the British during the assault on Quebec City. He was released in May 1776, and he returned to Connecticut and to the military. In 1777, he was promoted to colonel.

He became somewhat famous in May 1777 when he led a raid against the British forces in Sag Harbor, New York. With 220 men in a fleet of thirteen whaleboats, he crossed Long Island Sound from Connecticut to Long Island to attack the British fleet at night. The raid succeeded in burning twelve ships and taking 90 prisoners, without losing a single man, and the successful engagement became known as the "Meigs Raid." Later, the U.S. Congress awarded him a sword for his heroism. Meigs commanded a regiment under General Anthony Wayne at the Battle of Stony Point near today's Charleston, South Carolina.

At the conclusion of the war, Meigs was appointed a surveyor for the Ohio Company of Associates and assisted in the early settlement of Ohio. While it was still a territory, he served as a judge, justice of the peace and clerk of courts and was also a member of the General Assembly from 1799 to 1801.

In 1801, Meigs went to Tennessee to fill both the positions of agent to the Cherokee Nation and military agent for the United States War Department in East Tennessee. His first post was at the Cherokee Agency at Fort Southwest Point in what is now Kingston, but in 1807 he moved to a new post named Hiwassee Garrison, located near the mouth of the Hiwassee River. While at Southwest Point, Meigs was instrumental in negotiating with the Cherokees over the route and construction of the Old Federal Road. As Indian agent, Meigs promoted the rights of the Cherokees and defended them in treaty negotiations when he felt that the government was trying to manipulate them. He also worked to ensure that the Cherokees had plenty of corn during the lean years of 1814–15. Realizing the importance of laws and civility, he encouraged the Cherokees to establish a republican form

Above: Revolutionary War Patriot Return Jonathan Meigs was a retired war hero when he received his appointment as Indian agent to the Cherokees. Meigs served in this capacity from 1801 until his death in January 1823. He lived for a time in Calhoun, and the site of his house is marked on Main Street. *Author's collection.*

Below: Colonel Return J. Meigs is buried at the Old Garrison Cemetery near the Tennessee River in Rhea County, along with his son and second wife, Grace Starr Meigs. *Photo by Stephanie Guy.*

of government, which they eventually did. He also had a great effect on a young, half-Scottish, one-eighth Cherokee named John Ross.

He served as military agent until 1813, when the federal soldiers stationed at Hiwassee Garrison were withdrawn, but he continued as Cherokee agent on the Hiwassee River until his death. He is appropriately honored by Tennessee in two ways: Meigs County and Meigs Mountain in the Smokies both bear the name of the Revolutionary War veteran and friend of the Indians.

Cherokees in Charles Town, 1759

In the fall of 1759, the Cherokee Indians were deeply concerned about a trade embargo decreed by the South Carolina colonial governor, William Lyttelton, who was angered over some Indian attacks on his frontier. Within the past few years, the British had built two forts deep within the Cherokee lands: Fort Loudoun in the Overhill Country and Fort Prince George on the Keowee River in the Lowcountry. That September, a group of some thirty Cherokee chiefs left their towns and traveled southeast along the traders' path known as the "Northwest Passage" to meet with Governor Lyttelton in Charles Town.

The trail led from near present Vonore to Tellico Plains, Tennessee, through Unicoi Gap and then on through Murphy and Franklin, North Carolina, before passing over the uppermost tip of Georgia. The path then crossed the Chattooga River into South Carolina, where it led through present-day Clemson.

The Cherokees stopped at Fort Prince George before turning south near present Greenville. From here, the Cherokees would have more or less followed the general route of today's Interstate 26 running southwest through Laurens, Congaree, Dorchester and Moncks Corner. After a month of walking five hundred miles through the mountains and the South Carolina Lowcountry, the men arrived in Charles Town.

The Cherokees had found themselves dependent on the goods they acquired from the English traders and hoped that Lyttelton would be merciful to them. After all, they had no control over what a few angry young warriors had done in the spring under the influence of a French spy. All they wished was to be able to trade and live peaceably with their British neighbors, especially those stationed in the two frontier forts.

Along this road in the Appalachian Mountains, near Coker Creek, have passed the feet, wagons and automobiles of travelers for over one thousand years. The Northwest Passage, later called the Unicoi Turnpike, was the favored route of traders and Cherokee Indians when traveling between the Overhill Cherokee towns and Charleston, South Carolina. *Courtesy of Kathleen Dalton.*

Governor William Lyttelton, though, was an arrogant, overweight, pompous man with little regard for what he considered to be "savages." He was in no hurry to hold an audience with the chiefs, but at the behest of Lieutenant Governor William Bull, he finally agreed to see them. The Cherokees, led by the war chief Oconostota, were taken to the governor's room at the South Carolina Statehouse on Broad Street.

As was their custom, Oconostota directed two of the chiefs to bring up tokens of peace: several fine animal skins and strings of white beads. The Great Warrior then addressed Lyttelton through an interpreter: "Great Father, I present these skins as a token of peace, sent by Old Hop, the Little Carpenter, and others who wish to make the path straight, and brighten the chain, and accommodate our differences. It is our wish that you know the offenses which anger our Father were committed by young warriors provoked by the French. My people wish to—"

The author and his son, Jackson, at the Old South Carolina Statehouse in Charleston. This building housed colonial governor William Lyttelton's office in the summer of 1759 when a Cherokee delegation led by Chief Oconostota met with the governor on an ill-fated mission of peace. The meeting set in motion the events that would lead to the fall of Fort Loudoun the following summer. *Photo by Stephanie Guy.*

The governor then cut him off. "I will not accept these token of peace today," said Lyttelton dryly, "nor talk anymore of peace with the Cherokee." The Cherokees were shocked at the insult. But Lyttelton was not finished:

> *Many times I have heard the Cherokee say they are my friends. But time and time again your actions have proven differently. I see that you are only pretending to be deputed to me, but you are not.*
>
> *As you have at least attempted to come to Charlestown and make a show of friendship, you may return home. But I have in my hand a dispatch from the Commander at Fort Prince George, who writes clearly of the bad behavior of the Cherokee around him. Be it known to you and all these with you that I will soon lead a large force of my soldiers to your country, and then you will know the demands I have set for peace, and the satisfaction that I will require.*

Without a thought, Lyttelton directed his guards to show the Cherokees out.

The chiefs saw Lyttelton's threats clearly, and as they left the statehouse, they knew that bad times were on the horizon. Soon they found themselves placed under guard by the governor and held at Fort Prince George. Lyttelton's actions would eventually lead to what became known as the

Cherokee War, during which Forts Prince George and Loudoun were both put under siege by the Cherokees during the summer of 1760. Oconostota and a few others were able to gain their release, and when they attempted to rescue the remaining twenty-four chiefs at Fort Prince George, the English soldiers killed every Indian hostage. When the men and women at Fort Loudoun finally surrendered in August and left the fort to attempt to get back to Fort Prince George, the Cherokees attacked at Cane Creek near Tellico Plains, killing twenty-four people and taking the rest as prisoners. It was said that the twenty-four lives were to pay for the twenty-four chiefs taken prisoner by Lyttelton and killed at Fort Prince George.

Today, the old South Carolina Statehouse still stands on Broad Street in Charleston and is now used as the Charleston County Courthouse. It remains a part of the Fort Loudoun story, the place where an English colonial governor set in motion events that would cost the lives of both Cherokees and whites five hundred miles away in what would become East Tennessee.

Wilderness Survival in Eighteenth-century Tennessee: The James Smith Story

During colonial times, the early American frontier was a proving ground for rugged individualism and survival. A part of our American spirit of determination was born on the frontier, when our forefathers encountered a harsh wilderness and often unfriendly Indians. Only those men who were tenacious and resourceful enough managed to survive the frontier experience.

One such instance is recorded in the experiences of James Smith, a longhunter who accompanied a party of men into what is now Tennessee in the summer and fall of 1766. The men composed one of the first parties of longhunters ever recorded, and they explored and hunted over much of East and Middle Tennessee throughout the end of 1766 and well into 1767.

Upon reaching the mouth of the Tennessee on the Ohio in the summer of 1767, the group decided to head onward to the Illinois country—everyone, that is, except James Smith, who missed his wife and children and feared that he'd been gone so long that his wife would think him "killed by Indians." So he traded his horse to the other men for spare ball and powder and acquired the services of a mulatto slave, Jamie, who was with the party. The hunters parted on good terms, and James Smith and Jamie turned east.

The James Smith party left the Holston Settlements of southwest Virginia in 1766 on one of the first long hunts into the Tennessee country. Leaving the party to return the following year, Smith soon found himself injured. His knowledge of Indian woodcraft and his ability to work with the tools in his pouch allowed him to survive and return home. *Photo by Stephanie Guy.*

Eight days into their journey, though, Smith received a painful and debilitating wound when he stepped on a cane sliver that penetrated the sole of his moccasin and became lodged in his foot. Suddenly, Smith found himself incapacitated, with no horse to carry him and alone in the wilderness with only the supplies in his pack and Jamie to assist him.

The story of James Smith might have ended there, as it must surely have for many other men stranded and injured in the backcountry with less resolve and knowledge. But James Smith was an experienced woodsman. At only twenty-nine years of age, he had already fought numerous skirmishes with Indian war parties, endured five years of Indian captivity and ridden with the "Black Boys" who patrolled the North Carolina backwoods. Finding himself unable to travel and facing starvation, Indian capture and death, James Smith relied on his knowledge and experience to survive.

Knowing the importance of first tending to his serious injury, Smith pulled from his pack a leather awl, a knife and a bullet mold. With these impromptu surgical instruments, he managed to remove the sliver:

> *I struck the awl in the skin, and with the knife I cut away the flesh from around the cane and then I commanded the mulatto fellow to catch it with the bullit molds, and pull it out, which he did. When I saw it, it seemed a shocking thing to be in any person's foot; it will therefore be supposed that I was very glad to have it out.*

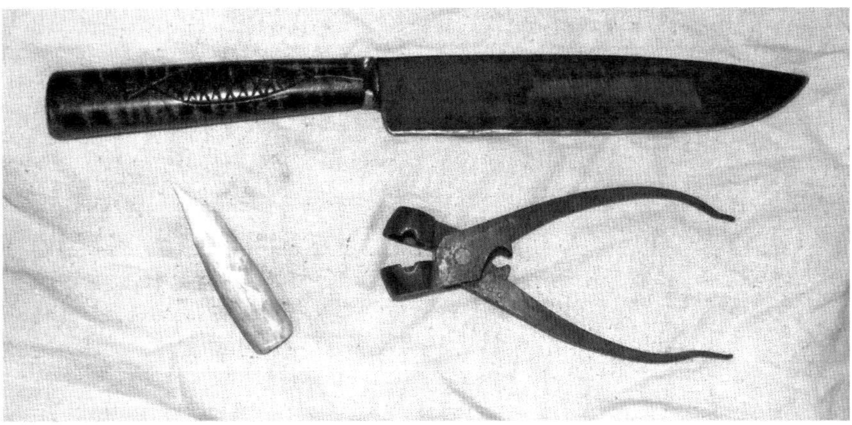

The tools James Smith found in his hunting pouch included his knife, a leather awl and a bullet mold. He was able to utilize the items as makeshift surgical tools with the help of his companion and slave, Jamie. *Photo by Stephanie Guy.*

Besides being extremely painful, the wound was surely deep. Realizing the danger of infection, Smith further instructed Jamie to

> *search for Indian medicine, and told him to get me a quantity of bark from the root of a lynn tree, which I made him beat on a stone with a tomahawk, and boil in a kettle, and with the ooze I bathed my foot and leg; what remained when I had finished bathing, I boiled to a jelly and made poultices thereof. As I had no rags, I made use of the green moss that grows upon logs, and wrapped it around with elm bark, by this means (simple as it may seem) the swelling and inflammation abated.*

During the summer, the "lynn" tree (linn, linden tree or basswood) would have been easy to find. Its blooms still would have been bright and fragrant, and the creamy white flowers are known to attract swarms of bees. Today, we are aware that linn trees contain certain compounds that are known to lower blood pressure and swelling and act as anesthetics. The fact that Smith boiled the jelly poultice would have provided him with a sterile dressing for his wound.

Still barely able to move, Smith noticed clouds moving in and saw the signs of a coming storm. He told Jamie to "make us a shelter, which he did by erecting forks and poles and covering them over with cane tops like a fodder house." This half-faced shelter, common among longhunters, would keep the two men and their gear comfortable and dry during Smith's convalescence.

Next came food. As he had situated his camp near a well-worn buffalo trail, Smith gave Jamie his gun. With Smith's instruction, Jamie was able to kill a buffalo and assisted the longhunter as they "jirked [dried over a low scaffold over a slow fire] the lean and fried the tallow out of the fat meat, which we kept to stew our jerk as we needed it."

But meat was not the only thing that Smith knew how to derive from the wildlife they killed. As they made their way slowly back to the east, Jamie's clothes began to wear out. According to Smith, Jamie eventually wore breechclout, leggings and moccasins of deer or elk hide, as well as a bearskin that was "dressed with the hair on which he belted around him."

Finally, three months after his injury, "seeing no bread, money, or spirituous liquors," James Smith and Jamie arrived back in the Yadkin River settlements. But his troubles were not over, for the wary North Carolina frontier people did not believe that the two strange men dressed in pelts and fur caps could have possibly survived such an ordeal to return safely over the mountains. Smith and Jamie were actually placed in jail for a time, until a friend supplied them with proper clothing that allowed the people to see them as normal men again.

The story of James Smith's wilderness survival during the summer of 1767 was remarkable at that time and still is today. It is interesting that Smith made do with what he had in his pack and with what medicines, food and clothing he could manufacture from the woods around him. Men like James Smith had taken the time to learn woodcraft and were able to make application of this knowledge. His story is a lesson in survival and self-reliance in the face of death and danger, far back on the frontier of history.

The Assassination of Jack Walker

Driving through one of the busiest intersections in Cleveland, Tennessee, few people have time to read the roadside historical marker on Highway 11 at Paul Huff Parkway. It marks the site of a home—and of at least one grave—and relates a murder story almost two centuries old.

John "Jack" Walker Jr. was one-quarter Cherokee Indian. His father was Major John Walker, a half-breed who had fought with Andrew Jackson in the Creek Wars in 1814. Major Walker had obtained a large amount of land along the Hiwassee River about 1800, calling it Walker's Ferry. When he signed the Treaty of 1816, he was so impressed with Secretary of War John C. Calhoun that Walker renamed his settlement "Calhoun." When it became a part of McMinn County in 1819, the first county court was held in Walker's home.

Jack Walker was born about 1800 at the Cherokee town of Wachowee. His father became an influential Cherokee leader, accumulated some wealth through land and business dealings and lived as prosperously as any whites at the time. Young Jack was able to attend school in New Jersey before returning to Tennessee. He was married on January 10, 1824, to Emily Stanfield Meigs, daughter of Return J. Meigs. As was the custom among Cherokees, he also had a Cherokee wife, Nannie Bushyhead. He obtained a large farm just north of present-day Cleveland and built a fine two-story home there.

Jack Walker grew to be a Cherokee leader, as his father had been, and was for a while a civil officer. During this time, he confiscated an illegal load

John Walker's two-story log house stood near this historical marker on Keith Street near Stuart Road in present-day Cleveland, Tennessee. When he was ambushed and shot by fellow Cherokees, he was brought back here to die. He was buried near the house, but his exact grave site has been lost. *Photo by Stephanie Guy.*

of whiskey from two other half-breeds on Conasauga River near the Georgia line. The names of the men were James Foreman and Anderson Springston.

In 1831, when the Cherokee Nation was faced with relocation encouraged by the federal government, Jack Walker traveled to Washington without the permission of the Cherokee Nation and advocated for Cherokee relocation, as he favored removal (as did most other wealthy half-breeds). His actions angered many Cherokees and made Walker several enemies. Still, he was outspoken in this regard, promoting the sale of Cherokee lands and moving west to the Oklahoma Territory. As the Cherokee Nation became divided over the issue, threats were made from the opposing sides. Some of the threats were directed at Jack Walker.

On August 24, 1834, Jack Walker attended a council meeting at Fort Morrow on the Federal Road in present-day Polk County. Again Walker engaged in some arguments over removal. That evening, he rode west back along present-day Benton Pike toward his home. He was accompanied by Dick Jackson of Athens. As they rode toward a large chestnut tree, a gun was fired, the bullet striking Walker in the left chest. Jackson would later identify two men whom he said he saw behind the tree: James Foreman and Anderson Springston. Jackson assisted in bringing Walker home, where he lingered for nineteen days before dying on September 11. The two assailants were soon arrested by McMinn County sheriff Spencer Beavers and placed in the jail at Athens, because Bradley County had not yet been formed and was still considered Indian land. They escaped but then were recaptured before standing trial.

The motive behind the shooting was, and is, debatable. It could have been retribution for Walker's advocacy for Cherokee removal, or it could simply have been personal revenge for Walker having formerly tangled with Foreman and Springston.

The trial was held initially at Athens, with the charges being dismissed on the grounds that a state court could not hold jurisdiction over a crime committed within the Cherokee Nation. This was overturned the following year by the Tennessee Supreme Court, and the ruling by Justice John Catron effectively took any power of Cherokee courts away, thus setting the stage for the "Trail of Tears."

Walker was buried behind his house, which was torn down in the 1930s with the widening of U.S. 11. Today, only the iron historical marker remains along Highway 11 in Cleveland, relating the tragic story of Jack Walker.

The Overbearing Governor

The story goes that in 1942, Nashville historian Stanley Horn was in a Philadelphia antiques shop when he found an old portrait of a dark-eyed man dressed in colonial-period clothing. On the back of the portrait, Horn found an inscription: "Major Joseph McMinn, painted at Philadelphia, 1796. R. Peale." Horn's discovery solved a mystery that many historians had struggled with for years: what did Joseph McMinn actually look like?

Even though today we can put a face to the governor who also gave McMinn County its name, it still puzzles historians as to exactly how Joseph McMinn ever got elected to be governor in the first place. He was not from an affluent family, did not have a large amount of wealth except for what he acquired working in his own fields himself and was no great orator, nor even a skilled politician. But one thing is clear: he was a man of determination, somewhat overbearing and more than a little sly. It certainly seems that these were the qualities that got him into the governor's office, and they are best seen in his dealings with the Cherokees.

Joseph McMinn was born to Quaker parents in Pennsylvania in 1758. In 1787, he married Hannah Cooper and moved to Hawkins County in what would become Tennessee. He worked the farm fields with his wife and, in 1790, joined the Hawkins County Militia, becoming a major and a justice of the peace. In 1796, McMinn was one of five delegates sent by Hawkins County to Knoxville to help draft the first state constitution, and throughout that January he worked alongside such men as Andrew Jackson and James Robertson. When it was ratified, McMinn was honored to be chosen to deliver the document to the U.S. secretary of state, Timothy Pickering, in Philadelphia. It was during this time that the thirty-eight-year-old McMinn very likely met George Washington and John Adams and had his portrait painted by Rembrandt Peale, who had also painted Washington's portrait.

Joseph McMinn, for whom McMinn County in Tennessee is named, served as governor of Tennessee from 1815 to 1821. For many years, no image of McMinn's face was thought to exist. In 1942, this portrait was found in an antique shop in Philadelphia. It was painted in 1796 when McMinn was a member of the Tennessee legislature and had brought the new state constitution to the U.S. Congress, which was still meeting in Philadelphia. The painting of then major McMinn was done by Rembrandt Peale. *Courtesy of the McMinn County Historical Society.*

Upon his return, he was elected colonel of the militia, followed by six terms in the Tennessee legislature, and he also served as speaker of the Senate. During this time, in 1811, his first wife died. He remarried the next year to eighteen-year-old Rebecca Kincade, who died three years later of a "nervous fever," followed two weeks later by the death of his daughter, Jane.

In the same year, 1815, he was approached by a group of citizens to run for governor. He would serve three terms, each time gaining a huge percentage of the vote. While governor, McMinn set himself to one particular task: removal of the Cherokees. He considered them a "set of vagrant hunters" and an "unprincipled foe."

Rather than employ others to negotiate with the Indians, McMinn went himself. He was not a healthy man, having a chronic stomach problem that Native American food particularly aggravated. But he went from town to town, gathering Cherokee chiefs together, calling councils and pushing the Cherokees toward leaving their lands to settle in the West. Often, chiefs would refuse to talk to him, whereupon he would camp nearby and daily press the chiefs for an audience until he got to speak to them. He was downright pushy, and looking back, it is a wonder that the Cherokees did not waylay and kill him on some remote trail.

After leaving the governor's office, McMinn was offered the position of agent to the Cherokee Indians. He came to Calhoun, in the county that bore his name, and worked to encourage the Cherokees to migrate west. He served as Indian agent here until dying suddenly at his desk in 1824. *Photo by Stephanie Guy.*

Finally, in June 1817, McMinn was successful in gathering a large number of Cherokees at Walker's Ferry (soon to be renamed Calhoun) on the Hiwassee River. It was the time of the Green Corn Dance, and McMinn had brought enough Cherokees together to arrange a council. He was assisted by General Andrew Jackson, who was just as tenacious as McMinn and who shared in the desire to remove the Cherokees. With enough chiefs present, McMinn and Jackson were able to get a treaty signed to encourage any Cherokees willing to go west by providing them with a "rifle gun and ammunition, a blanket, one brass kettle, or in lieu of a brass kettle, a beaver trap."

Throughout the rest of his tenure as governor, McMinn continued to make trips to the Cherokee country and encouraged the Hiwassee Purchase, which took place in 1818. When some counties were formed out of the purchased land in 1819, one of them bore his name.

He left the governor's office in 1821 and divorced his last wife, Nancy Williams, when she would not go with him back to Hawkins County. In

1823, at age sixty-five, he moved to Calhoun and returned to government service as an Indian agent, dying at his desk a year later, alone except for "his faithful body servant Dave," still working tirelessly to expel the Indians from Tennessee.

Part III
The Civil War

Besides our Cherokee history, the Civil War period has been overdramatized, misinterpreted and misrepresented in Southeast Tennessee. Deeply divided loyalties, Union-leaning counties with large slave populations and almost daily skirmishing were facts of life in the region during the war years. Here are stories you will likely never see in history books.

"They Killed Him at Goodsprings"

Some years after the Civil War, about 1870, a Union pension was filed on behalf of the late Lieutenant Colonel "Fighting" Joe Divine of Monroe County. The pension was mailed in by Thomas Boyd of Sweetwater on behalf of Joe Divine's widow, stating that Divine had died of smallpox and that as a Union soldier his widow was due the pension. However, this would prove to be a complete fabrication when it was investigated in 1876. Divine's pension application was part of a scheme by Thomas Boyd, a former Confederate officer, to defraud the federal government of Union pensions. The allegation of Divine's death by smallpox was a lie and hid the sad truth of the fate of Joe Divine.

Joe Divine was born in South Carolina in 1812 and later moved to the Big Creek community of Monroe County, Tennessee. He was forty-nine years old when the Civil War began, so Joe was not as passionate as many of his younger neighbors to enter into the fight. In fact, it would be late in the war before Joe became active, and like many older men in East Tennessee, Joe made the decision to join the Union cause.

In the summer of 1864, he received a commission as lieutenant colonel from Governor Andrew Johnson and was ordered to organize a regiment of Union volunteers for one hundred days' service. Divine organized a brigade of the Third Mounted Tennessee Infantry, United States, at Loudon in August 1864 to operate in the area of Loudon and Monroe Counties. The men in the Third Tennessee were a rough lot; most were deserters from both the Confederate and Union armies. They were often desperate men, looking for a way to protect themselves from prosecution or to get even with neighbors with opposing political views. Some had been outright outlaws—several former members of Monroe County's Confederate-leaning "Kirkland Bushwhackers" even joined up. The

Above, left: Joe Divine was an East Tennessee Unionist who fell afoul of his Confederate neighbors in Monroe County due to his "bushwhacker" tactics. Kidnapped from Madisonville, he was held for several days before being found murdered in the Goodsprings community in McMinn County. His grave is at Big Springs Cemetery in Monroe County. *Photo by Stephanie Guy.*

Above, right: At the foot of Joe Divine's grave is this monument, which relates that he was "tortured and murdered by rebel soldiers." *Photo by Stephanie Guy.*

Somewhere near these crossroads, in the Goodsprings community of McMinn County, Joe Divine was murdered. He was buried in a nearby field. His family later had his remains brought back to Big Springs in Monroe County. *Photo by Stephanie Guy.*

fact that these men joined Divine is a deep indication that he shared in their thirst for revenge and plunder.

Divine's Battalion, as it became known, saw little actual battlefield fighting. The most notable conflict the soldiers took part in was a skirmish with members of Thomas's Confederate Cherokee Legion at Robbinsville, North Carolina, in November. But the presence and activities of Divine's Union battalion did not sit well with Confederates in Monroe County. The fact that several former Confederates now served under the Union flag certainly did little to endear Divine and his men to his Monroe County neighbors, and this was especially infuriating as the war wound down and a Union victory became apparent. After the one hundred days of service had been fulfilled, the enlisted men of the Third Mounted Infantry were mustered out in December, with the officers, including Divine, being mustered out on January 4, 1865. By this time, Divine was serving as deputy provost marshal for Monroe County. It seems that the bitter Confederates in Monroe County decided that with Divine and his fellow officers no longer officially soldiers, it was time to extract some vengeance of their own. Within weeks, several of the regiment's officers were hunted down and killed.

It had only been a few days since being relieved of his command, in January 1865, when Joe Divine learned from friends that he was marked for death. He hid for a while in the cellar of Dr. Upton on Main Street in Madisonville (later the Bierely Funeral Home), and it was there that he was found and captured by Monroe County Confederates. They held him for several days, and perhaps fearing that his friends would try to free him, he was taken south to the Goodsprings area of McMinn County. It was there that his captors grew tired of him, and he was viciously beaten to death on January 28. Others say that he was shot. Divine was buried in a field until his family moved his remains to Big Creek Cemetery. His headstone there notes that he was "tortured and murdered by rebel soldiers." It had been twenty-four days since he'd been mustered out.

Divine could not escape the turmoil that was the Civil War in East Tennessee and learned firsthand that one had to choose his path wisely in those days, when some allegiances were deep and others shifted with the winter wind. Although he saw little action on the battlefield, his own blood would be shed even as the war was coming to an end, a victim of his own desire to extract revenge against his neighbors.

WHERE THE TRAVELERS RESTED

In 1829, Tom Rogers built a two-story house near the north bank of the Hiwassee River in the small settlement of Calhoun. At the time, the place was still a frontier town, having only been known as Calhoun for about ten years. It had for some time before been the lands belonging to a Cherokee, John Walker, who operated a ferry near the location of Rogers's house. But as the town was growing due to an increase in population, Tom Rogers saw an opportunity: travelers needed a place to rest and get a good meal. So he added to his home additional rooms and a good kitchen and called the place a tavern.

A few years earlier, Calhoun had been the county seat of McMinn County, but by the time Rogers began operating his tavern, the county seat had been moved about fifteen miles north, to a place on Eastanaulee Creek they were calling Athens. But Calhoun remained an important location: it was a place to cross the lazy Hiwassee and also afforded one of the last river ports upstream from where the Hiwassee joined the Tennessee. Rogers certainly must have done good business. A few notable patrons are associated with those early days, like Cherokee leaders Johns and Lewis Ross and, of course, John Walker. Then there was John Howard Payne, who spent time at the hotel in 1836. He would later write a well-known song that some believe referred to his stay at the Rogers Tavern, called "Home Sweet Home."

Travelers arrived by either the dirt road that ran north–south or by canoe or flatboat on the river. Tavern rooms were small and efficient, with only a bed and dry sink—little more than a place to sleep and wash off a bit of the sweat and dust from the trail. Guests would often arrive in the late afternoon or evening, clean up and then gather in a large dining room for the evening meal.

It was customary in a frontier tavern for all guests to take supper together around one table. This allowed for less work for the staff, which probably consisted of Mr. Rogers's family and maybe a few slaves. It was also an opportunity for travelers to meet one another and trade news they had heard on the river or the road. Was there still good land left for sale? Are the roads safe to travel? We heard that some people were robbed and killed coming down from Athens. Will the Cherokees sell any more land? Are they going to move west? Where do you hail from—did you say the Nolichucky? Ah, yes, my father was with Mr. Brown back in '77, when the Indians came…

Of all the guests who enjoyed the hospitality of Rogers Tavern, the most well known seem to be associated with the Civil War. In a recent presentation to the McMinn County Historical Society, Calhoun city manager Joe Bryan referred to stories written by C.L. McAlister several years ago.

Calhoun was still an important place in the 1860s, for in addition to a ferry it had also acquired a railroad bridge, and both Union and Confederate forces passed over its tracks. Colonel Nathan Bedford Forrest fought a small skirmish there, driving back some Yankee cavalry in 1862, right through Rogers's yard. In late 1863, General James Longstreet and his staff left Chattanooga, headed for a coming battle at Fort Sanders in Knoxville and are believed to have stayed at the Rogers Tavern. So goes an indication that Generals U.S. Grant and William Sherman stayed there soon afterward. A rather detailed account refers to Confederate general Braxton Bragg, who was familiar with Major McConnell, Captain Lafferty and Captain Dill, who were all residents of Calhoun and who joined Bragg with their wives for a "gala night" at the tavern.

Plugs were placed in the floor of the old house, for the plugs were removed when the temperamental Hiwassee flooded—this would allow the water to flow into and not against the house, keeping it from floating away.

The building stood for many years, although a past owner tore off the top story to enlarge the bottom floor and changed the front of the house to the rear, which today faces Main Street. Once a focal point of the river town, it sat as a squat, white frame house on what is now industrial property, quietly hiding its history of travelers, Indians and generals. Sadly, the old tavern burned to the ground in 2007, erasing the last physical evidence of its significance.

UNCLE PAT

I searched through Hammonds Cemetery, knowing that he was there somewhere. It was hot, and I only had a few minutes before an afternoon meeting. As I walked along, quietly searching the stones, huge crows began to fill a large oak overhead. I ignored them at first, but I could feel their black eyes watching me. Finally, there he was. Almost one hundred years old when he died, his headstone sways sideways like an old man's leanings. But the words, unlike many in the old cemetery, remained clear: "Patrick Spriggs, Co C, 42nd Regt US Cld Inf."

I wiped away some sweat, and loud enough for the crows to hear, I said, "Hello, Uncle Pat."

Born a slave on July 28, 1849, Pat Spriggs was probably owned by Ezekiel Spriggs, of McMinn and (later) Bradley Counties. Since most landowners did not own slaves in Southeast Tennessee, Ezekiel must have been quite wealthy. Pat was likely a field hand and lived the life of a slave for fifteen years. Then came the Civil War, and along with the comings and goings of both Confederates and Unionists were demands for slave labor. This was true on both sides, and slave owners were compensated for the army's use of their slaves. The Emancipation Proclamation, in truth, did not free any slaves at all; it only declared the slaves in the Confederate-held areas as free. Slaves in the Union-held areas remained in bondage, and so by 1864 Pat was still a slave in Union-held Bradley County.

"Uncle" Pat Spriggs as an old man. The former Bradley County slave eventually became a soldier in the Union army during the Civil War. *Author's collection.*

One can imagine that this ironic situation must have frustrated many slaves, and it is no surprise to find that Pat ran away from the Spriggs farm that summer. It appears that he went south to Chattanooga, where white Union officers were recruiting black

Pat Spriggs, black Civil War veteran, was held in deep respect among both white and black citizens in McMinn County. His military headstone is located at Hammonds Cemetery in Athens. *Photo by Stephanie Guy.*

men as soldiers, and Pat signed on with the Forty-second Regiment, U.S. Colored Troops, under Captains Williams and Middleton. But fearful of his status as a runaway slave, Pat enrolled under the name of Patrick Murphy.

There remained much debate about black troops, but as a rule the different regiments performed as well as any white military units. In his own accounts, Pat related his service in two skirmishes at Dalton, Georgia, and at Sand Mountain; according to records, he served with honor. Although blacks had served with distinction as early as the Revolutionary War, it must have been a sobering sight for many white Southerners to see entire regiments of black soldiers marching through Southern towns, the first time such a thing had been done in the United States.

Besides the incidents at Dalton and Sand Mountain, the Forty-second provided guards and laborers for numerous duties during the course of its service, which ran as late as January 1866, when Pat was discharged.

He returned to McMinn County, where he lived out the rest of a long life. He met his wife, Jane Wiles Spriggs—also a former slave who had been brought to Athens at the close of the war—and they raised two children. Pat apparently owned a restaurant in the area of North White Street for some time, and through his daily life in Athens he became a well-respected member of the community. He was a charter member of the local Grand

Army of the Republic (GAR) Post, which is remarkable since many posts nationwide did not accept blacks and whites together. At the ripe old age of ninety-seven, Pat passed away in Athens.

His funeral made the front page of the *Post-Athenian* on August 20, 1936: "Aged Negro Vet of Union Army Dies in Athens." The funeral, held at the Cumberland Presbyterian Church, was attended equally by blacks and whites. Pat's coffin was draped with the American flag, and a long procession followed it through town to its interment in Hammonds Cemetery.

There he sleeps, alongside other black veterans of American wars. But men like Pat were among the first, and his leaning headstone hides this fact. As does the grass in Hammonds Cemetery that now covers an unknown number of slaves buried there who never knew the freedom for which Pat and his fellow soldiers in the "Colored" ranks fought, unseen except for the black eyes of the crows that keep a cautious vigil over the occasional visitor.

"THE YANKS HAVE FORTIFIED THE COURTHOUSE"

It was an act of desperation to begin with, and it would bring nothing but failure, but to Confederate general John Bell Hood, it made perfect sense. In July 1864, Hood was backed up against Atlanta with Union general W.T. Sherman literally in his face. Hood called for the commander of his cavalry, Joe Wheeler, to ride into the rear of Sherman, cutting the railroads and supply lines, which would hopefully turn Sherman's attention away from Atlanta. On August 10, twenty-seven-year-old Wheeler set out with four thousand men in the saddle.

Wheeler's objective was to attack the Western and Atlantic Railroad south of Chattanooga and then move into Middle Tennessee and strike the railroads there. He was to leave about half of his force in Tennessee to continue to make trouble for the Yanks and then return to Hood for a strike against Sherman.

At first, the raid was successful, as Wheeler's troops destroyed some thirty miles of track between Marietta and Dalton. But then a large Union force drove him out of North Georgia completely, and contrary to orders, he was forced into Southeast Tennessee. One of the men who was with Wheeler was John C. Williamson, of Polk County. Williamson kept a diary of the raid that provides an insightful contemporary account of the end of the war in East Tennessee.

Williamson speaks of the daily trials of a cavalryman, how his horse, Kit, gave out on August 12 and how he swapped him for a new horse called Rozenantee. His patrol made its way north, camped near Frog Town on the Old Federal Road and then camped along the Coosawattee River the following night. His description of the situation in Walker County was typical of North Georgia and Southeast Tennessee: "The bushwhackers have been having everything their own way, taking any kind of property they want and dividing it among themselves."

Williamson visited his father and then fought a pitched battle around Dalton before being driven back almost to Cleveland on the fifteenth, and he then turned and rode into Benton. Here the men "pressed" several horses, meaning they took mounts from the citizens. He wrote, "The people had not heard of our coming and had not hid their horses."

It is interesting how Williamson found that his Confederate neighbors had changed since the beginning of the war. Polk County had voted overwhelmingly for secession in 1861, but Williamson seemed disappointed in what he saw: "Everybody has taken the oath. They seem to avoid the Rebels. Very different from three years ago."

At about 10:00 a.m. on the sixteenth, the patrol crossed the Hiwassee at Savannah Farms. Williamson was given a pair of socks by the wife of one of his former neighbors, P.B. Mayfield, but the lady insisted that he "tell no one lest the Yankees get hold of it." On the seventeenth, he related the capture of Newt Coe, a Union bushwhacker, along with some of Coe's brothers. On the eighteenth, the patrol rode through Columbus and struck the Athens Road, heading north into McMinn County. But the difficulty of maintaining its prisoners was evident that night when Williamson simply wrote, "Newt Coe got away."

At 10:00 a.m. the following morning, the patrol reached Riceville and commenced to burning the railroad, tearing up seven miles of it and camping just south of Athens, where a heavy rain began to fall. He continued:

> *Aug 20: We left camp about two hours by sun. The railroad is still being burned. I got breakfast in Athens at Henry Parks place. I stopped at Blizzards. He was gone. His wife was very kind to us. Our boys have robbed Athens and have robbed some good Southern people. J. Horton has gone north. The Yanks have fortified the courthouse. Harbison could have taken the place at any time. There were only forty yanks in the place. All the cord wood south of Athens has been burned. From Athens we came to Sweetwater and destroyed the railroad all the way.*

Above: Riding north from Polk County, Confederate cavalryman John C. Williamson recorded that his patrol took the Athens Road into McMinn County with the mission to burn the railroad. The old road passed directly in front of this residence in the Claxton community, now the Edna Pickens residence. The Rebel cavalry would have ridden along the original road visible in the foreground. *Photo by Stephanie Guy.*

Left: The East Tennessee and Georgia Railroad followed the present roadbed of Southern Railway through McMinn County. According to John C. Williamson, this area of track north of Riceville was torn up and burned in an effort to disturb the Union-held area. *Photo by Stephanie Guy.*

Another account of the same series of days is given by Union brigadier general Jacob Ammen:

> *The 18th of August I retired to Knoxville, and as there were rumors of the enemy at Athens, proceeded on the morning train to Loudon (19th), and put a strong guard (ninety-five) on the train, which proceeded within three miles of Athens, where it was attacked by such a force as to render it expedient to return, our forces returning the fire and preventing the capture of the train. Two of our men were slightly wounded; no other injury.*

This may have also been the same instance recorded by J.M. Sharp:

> *The Yankees in the courthouse fought so well the Rebels left. After the war there wasn't a hog or a rail fence around the town. The railroad had been torn up and the people were in a bitter mood.*

Eventually, Williamson's patrol was able to connect back with the rest of Wheeler's forces and moved on into Middle Tennessee. Wheeler destroyed some railroads but was harassed nearly the entire time and barely made it back to Hood in Atlanta. His command was so damaged that he could not resume any operations until that October.

The whole affair was in vain. Hood had only sacrificed a necessary cavalry force, while Sherman's men were able to repair the railroads almost as soon as they were torn up. Perhaps the most important piece of information that Wheeler reported to Hood was the fact that Nashville was well defended by Union general Thomas. But Hood ignored this information and, after Atlanta fell, marched north on his fateful invasion of Tennessee, where he found only destruction at Franklin in November and Nashville in December. After the war, Wheeler became a general in the U.S. Army, the only man to serve both as a Confederate general and U.S. general.

The Price of War: The Van Dyke Sons

The Van Dyke House in Athens, known historically as Prospect Hill, was during a greater part of the nineteenth century the home of Judge Thomas Nixon Van Dyke and his family. The house still stands behind the old Whiteway Shopping Center and is a focus of interest in the history surrounding the Van Dyke family.

Much of Judge Van Dyke's life was full of success: a fine home, a large family, a busy law practice, a position as clerk of the Alabama House of Representatives, an election as chancellor and work as a businessman. But the family also endured a great amount of heartbreak and loss, especially during the Civil War.

First of all, the Van Dykes were Confederates in deeply divided East Tennessee, and while the Confederacy held sway over McMinn County, the family continued to prosper. But when the Union army came, their fortunes were reversed. Van Dyke's home was used to house Union officers, his property was confiscated and in January 1864 he was sent to prison at Camp Chase, Ohio. When General Sherman occupied the Van Dyke home later that year, he issued passes for the Van Dyke women to move north. It was not until after the war that Judge Van Dyke gained his release and found his family living in Wisconsin—much to their relief, as it had been rumored that he had died. They then moved to Quincy, Illinois, before returning to their home in Athens in 1866.

Perhaps the most difficult of all the trials faced by Judge Van Dyke during the war was the fate of three of his sons. His four oldest boys fought in the war: William, John, Richard and Thomas. The youngest, Robert D., was born during the war. William, John and Richard all served in the Fifty-ninth Tennessee Mounted Infantry, and only William, who was a major in the commissary, survived the war. These three brothers all served with Captain Reuben Clark, a close family friend from Knoxville. Years after the war, Clark wrote his memoirs, *Valleys of the Shadow*. It is clear in the book that Clark considered the Van Dykes close friends, and in it Clark reveals that he was with both John and Richard when they were killed.

In July 1864, the Fifty-ninth was in the area of Darksville, Virginia. Heavy fighting was a day-to-day affair, and little time was given for relaxation. During one of the lulls, Captains Clark and John Van Dyke were invited to dinner by Ms. Broughton, a local girl in Darksville. After dinner, they learned that Yankees had invaded the town, and the two men rode to their commands. Just as they reached their lines, the Yankees charged, and Captain John Van Dyke fell, mortally wounded. He was placed in an ambulance, in which he soon died. He was carried back to Darksville and was buried under the direction of Ms. Broughton, with whom he had just been a guest. Clark wrote, "Thus ended the life of a modest, refined, and gallant young gentleman, whom I greatly esteemed."

Prospect Hill, home of the Thomas Nixon Van Dyke family, was built in 1834 by Dr. Thomas Deaderick, Van Dyke's father-in-law. Still a privately owned residence, it remains perhaps McMinn County's most historically significant home. *Author's collection.*

Two weeks later, the Fifty-ninth was near Lynchburg, and Clark went along with Lieutenant Richard "Dick" Van Dyke to get something to eat at a local home. Again, upon their return to their commands, they were charged by Union cavalry. Lieutenant Van Dyke was slightly wounded in the knee and joked with Clark: "Do you suppose I can get a furlough on this wound?" Unfortunately, the lieutenant's knee became infected, and he died soon after in Lynchburg. Clark wrote, "I have often thought of the coincidence of having dined for the last time with these two noble brothers and close friends of mine."

Last was Thomas, who volunteered for service in the Sixty-third Tennessee Infantry. While serving near Cumberland Gap, he became ill from exposure while on a mission to Kentucky. Wishing to return home to recover, he was allowed to do so, but his sickness grew worse, and he died on February 3, 1863, at Prospect Hill. His body was carried over to the family cemetery nearby and was buried there beside his sister, Letitia.

Young Thomas Van Dyke, buried beside his parents at the Athens Cedar Grove Cemetery. He was the youngest of Thomas Nixon Van Dyke's sons and the first to lose his life in the Civil War. Before the war ended, two more Van Dyke sons would lie beneath the earth in Virginia. *Photo by Stephanie Guy.*

This was the price the Van Dykes paid: three of their five sons lost in war. Both John's and Richard's bodies remained in Virginia, leaving only young Thomas's grave to be visited by his family at the cemetery that would eventually become Cedar Grove. Three sons, their blood spilled in the service of the Confederacy and their stories intertwining with the old mansion that still stands nearby within sight of a gathering of old headstones.

Daphney's Thanksgiving

Daphney stood in line with the other black children as the white people stood and looked at them. She had been sold before, when she was about eight, way down in Charleston in South Carolina. That day was burned into her memory—the day she was taken away from her mother and her brothers, Samuel and William. Daphney had cried and cried, and before the white man bought her and put her in his wagon, Mama kept talking to her, telling her to be a good girl and say her prayers and to remember who she was. She kept saying, "Don't cry, now, don't you cry now," like

The old Slave Mart in Charleston, South Carolina. Thousands of enslaved Africans were sold here, and it is possible that Daphney passed through this human market as a child when she was taken from her mother and brothers far away to East Tennessee. *Photo by Stephanie Guy.*

she would see her the next day. But Daphney had not seen her family for two years, and she was now being taken up through Georgia and to Athens, Tennessee.

When she was little, in Charleston, she and her family had been owned by the Edwardses, and Daphney was taught how to be a little nursemaid to the Edwards family's babies. She liked it, getting to hold and change the babies and getting to play with them. It made her feel big, like Mama. Daphney was really smart, so smart that one of the older Edwards girls had taught her how to read and do arithmetic. But Mama told her to keep quiet about it—a slave wasn't supposed to know how to do such things. Daphney had only disappointed Mr. Edwards once, when she dropped some eggs she'd been told to gather. He had hit her across the face with a stick, and she still carried the scar from his anger.

This morning, she had read a paper that the slave seller was writing and saw that the year was 1860 and that the place of sale was Athens, Tennessee. She did not know exactly where that was, but she knew that she was up above Charleston a long ways. Without Mama, she'd had to get on and learn to be a big girl, and so now she only cried late at night when she dreamed of Mama's face.

The slave seller had gotten her up early this morning, given her a clean dress and told her to clean her face and hands and fix her hair. She did like she was told and was brought into town in a wagon with some other slaves. They were made to stand in the dirt in front of the old brick courthouse, and one by one they were brought up to stand on a box to be bid on. Like before, Daphney had to do her tricks: show her teeth, jump up and down and smile,

Daphney Chestnut Melton Howard is pictured here as an adult. After working through the Civil War as a slave on the Peck farm in McMinn County, Daphney obtained her freedom. But this story of family separation would take a turn that remains one of the most touching sagas in McMinn County's history. *Courtesy of Ann Boyd.*

and she let the white people look her over, just like the slave seller had told her to do. Good people will buy you if you look happy, he had said. He walked around her as the white people gawked at her, telling them what a good girl she was, how she was no trouble at all and that she was ten years old and already a trained nursemaid.

A man named Peck bought her, put her in his wagon with his wife and took her way out in McMinn County to his farm. It was a big farm, and there was a big mountain she could see from the Peck house. Mrs. Peck told her that it was called Starr's Mountain and that Indians used to live in this valley.

For the next five years, she cooked and cleaned, worked in the garden and fields and sometimes was even a nurse when someone got sick. She would sometimes be sent to nearby houses with medicine, which she carried in a small basket. A war came, and both gray and blue soldiers roamed up and down the valley between the farm and the mountain. Soldiers paid them little mind, except when they were hungry, and Daphney would cook them a little food, too, if there was any. Most of the time Daphney took care of the Peck children. Sometimes, when the little ones would crawl up onto Mrs. Peck's lap, Daphney thought of her own mother. She tried hard to remember her family, never wanting to forget their faces or the sounds of their voices. But with the years going by, it was harder and harder to do. Mrs. Peck was a kind woman, and sometimes Daphney would tell her about Mama and how much she missed her.

She was about fifteen when Mr. Peck came to her one day and told her that she was free. The war was almost over, and slaves were all going to be freed, he said. Besides, times had gotten so hard that he couldn't afford to feed his own family, much less her. He told her that she could stay with them if she wished, and since she had nowhere else to go, she did. But there was something about Mr. Peck that seemed to change, and one day in November he called her to the house, where a strange man was sitting outside in a wagon. Mr. Peck told her she had been a good girl but that she must go with the man in the wagon, whose name was Chestnut. She took her few belongings, placed them in her basket and climbed in.

Mr. Chestnut seemed kind, and he talked to her as they rode along in the cool November afternoon. He asked her about her name and how old she was, and then he asked her about her family. He just smiled and listened as she talked about Mama, William and Samuel. She talked and talked, sometimes unconsciously touching the scar on her forehead, and before she knew it the wagon was coming up on Mr. Chestnut's farm on the Connector Road. Daphney guessed that it was not ten miles from the Peck farm.

Mr. Chestnut smiled, pointed to a little house out in the field and told her to take her things there. He told her that a Negro family was already living there but that they would not mind her staying, too. In fact, he said, you might know them.

Daphney walked toward the house with her bag. She saw two boys outside, and then she saw a woman holding a pot step into the doorway. She stepped closer and saw the pot drop from the woman's hands.

"Daphney?" said Mama. "Oh, my sweet, baby…is it you, Daphney?"

Daphney could not speak. The basket had fallen from her trembling hands, and for a moment she thought she was dreaming. Tears rolled down her cheeks as Mama and William and Samuel ran to her, embracing her.

Note: Many thanks are due to the family of the late Mrs. Dorothy Hitchcock and for her personal memories of her grandmother, Daphney Chestnut Melton Howard.

Forrest's Battle at Calhoun

Newspaper reports from the 1860s provide a window to the deep division and almost constant upheaval of communities. The reports from McMinn County are typical for much of the region, where few large-scale battles were fought but instead conflict continued on a smaller scale:

ATHENS POST, *FEBRUARY 16, 1861*
Athens: Sentiment seems to be running high here against seceding from the Union. In a recent series of elections to select delegates to State conventions the Union ticket has swept the field.

ATHENS POST, *MAY 24, 1861*
Mouse Creek (now Niota): A resolution passed here on May 18 has supported the state of Tennessee in its move to separate from the Northern Union. The resolution read: "That the war proclamation of Abraham Lincoln, the tyrant and usurper at Washington, meets with our unqualified disapprobation: that if carried, would lead to the subjugation of the 15 Southern states and that we will resist it to the direst extremity." Additional resolutions were composed to support Governor Isham Harris in his efforts toward Tennessee's secession, and the local troops who made up Captain H.B. Yearwood's Homeguard were also present in uniform, declaring they were ready to go to battle if needed.

ATHENS UNION POST, *SEPTEMBER 17, 1863*
Athens: The first edition of the Athens Union Post, *being published here by the Union Army, went on sale today. The paper has for its motto: "The Union Must and Shall Be Preserved."*

The publisher for the short-lived paper was Lieutenant N. Smith Boynton. The paper went on to call for volunteers from East Tennessee to join the Union army. Further stories included the action at the Hiwassee River Bridge in Calhoun, where Union forces recently driven from Cleveland had managed to stall attacking Confederates. After the war, the Southern-leaning Sam Ivins returned to Athens and resumed as the publisher.

This retreat of Union troops occurred after the Battle at Chickamauga, as Confederates tried to spread the effects of this victory northward and drive the Union army under General Burnside from Knoxville and out of East Tennessee. On September 26, General Nathan Bedford Forrest arrived on the south bank of the river at Charleston. He did not appreciate the fact that Federals across the river in Calhoun had slowed down the advance of his troops.

He gathered his men around him and gave them the plan of battle. Some of Forrest's men had served under General John Hunt Morgan, who had recently been captured and was being held in Columbus, Ohio. Forrest told his men, "Remember, boys, your commanding officer is now in a felon's cell. Let Morgan be your watchword, and give the Yankees hell."

The present railroad bridge spanning the Hiwassee River connects Charleston and Bradley Counties to the south with Calhoun and McMinn Counties to the north, and it sits on the original site of the Civil War–era bridge. The bridge was burned in 1861 and, after being rebuilt, was the site of a spirited charge on September 21, 1864, by General Nathan Bedford Forrest. Forrest's cavalry dislodged Union soldiers entrenched on the Calhoun side of the river in his efforts to follow up the Confederate victory at Chickamauga. *Photo by Stephanie Guy.*

The Union men were in positions on either side of the railroad bridge and had built a large blockhouse on the Calhoun side of the tracks for the protection of the bridge, which had been burned two years earlier. With his artillery firing from the heights around Charleston, Forrest tossed cannon shells across the Hiwassee into the Union entrenchments and blockhouse. Some damage was also inflicted on the nearby academy building, later the Masonic Hall, with an entire wall being blown away. Forrest stormed across the river and the railroad bridge to push the bluecoats out of Calhoun and toward Athens. Not long afterward, some of his troops routed a small Union force at Philadelphia just north of Sweetwater. On September 30, while still at Athens, Forrest was ordered by General Braxton Bragg, for whom Forrest had little regard, to turn over his entire cavalry force to General Joe Wheeler. He stormed back to Bragg's headquarters in Chattanooga and requested to be transferred to West Tennessee. The Confederate loss at Fort Sanders in Knoxville, and Grant's advancement from Chattanooga, ended the major Confederate operations in East Tennessee. Even so, in August 1864, men under Joe

Wheeler's command moved up from North Georgia, through Cleveland and Benton, and were again in downtown Athens for an all-day skirmish with Union cavalry barricaded in the courthouse.

Forrest never returned to Athens during the war and is recorded to have only been in McMinn County one other time at the beginning of the conflict. In 1862, while still a colonel, he camped his cavalry just outside of Athens at Cedar Grove Cemetery.

Part IV
Ghosts, Graves and Other Strange Happenings

Of all the stories I collect and research, the "spooky" ones are the most fun. Even when taking a photograph for a normal history story, sometimes strange images will appear in the picture, especially around old houses or in cemeteries. Some stories simply can't be explained, while others are easily debunked, but they all make for some great entertainment when mixed with a little factual history.

A Mausoleum, a Legend, a School and Angelina

Getting people to talk about ghost stories in the fall is like talking about football: if you're not careful, they'll tell you more than you want to know. A few more short summaries of area ghost stories will round out more hidden history, and a few of these are a bit different. It's easy to believe in a ghost story when it's associated with a grave, a mausoleum or an old, spooky house. Ghost stories involving hospitals and schools are something else.

Driving down Ocoee Street into downtown Cleveland brings most people to one of Bradley County's most haunted sites: the Craigmiles Mausoleum, which sits beside St. Luke's Episcopal Church.

The story behind the resting place of the Craigmiles family is associated with more tragedy than most families could endure. The mausoleum and, actually, the church itself were both built for little seven-year-old Nina

The Craigmiles family mausoleum in Cleveland, Tennessee. This Gothic structure holds the remains of several members of the family, including the body of little Nina Craigmiles. Her tragic death is part of the ghost story surrounding the mausoleum. *Photo by Stephanie Guy.*

Craigmiles. She was the daughter of Robert Craigmiles, wealthy Cleveland resident, and she was killed when the wagon in which she was riding ran in front of a passing train. Later, another Craigmiles child died, as did Mr. Craigmiles after falling on some ice. Over the years, strange red streaks have appeared on the sides of the mausoleum, and it has been said that a young girl dressed in nineteenth-century clothing has been seen standing nearby. It is also told that, at times, crying is heard in the area, which is attributed to little Nina looking for someone with whom she can play.

Another story revolves around forms being seen near the legendary Nocatula Grave on the campus of Tennessee Wesleyan College in Athens. This, of course, is tied to the supposed Cherokee girl who took her life when she discovered that her true love, a white soldier who took the name Conestoga, had been murdered by a rival Cherokee. According to the legend, the two young lovers were buried there, and in their cold hands were placed an acorn and a hackberry, both of which grew into two huge trees that dominated the campus for more than one hundred years. Students and faculty have long told stories of seeing the ghosts of the two tragic characters that "haunt" the campus.

What about a ghost in Etowah City School? Well, that's what some say. Unexplained occurrences such as voices heard in hallways and locker rooms, lights turning on and off, basketballs being dumped from racks and papers mysteriously torn off bulletin boards have all occurred either overnight or when no one else was found to be around. Some people claim that it is a ghost of a past student or faculty member, perhaps left from the old Etowah High School that once stood on the same site.

This last tale, though, is perhaps the eeriest. For many years, the maintenance and nursing staff at Woods Memorial Hospital in Etowah have talked about what many believe is the ghost of a nurse that haunts the hospital's patient wing. She is seen walking down the hallways, dressed in a white nurse's uniform, only to be seen at a glance as she passes in and out of rooms, as if checking on a patient, usually after a cool breeze passes through

This historical sign on the campus of Tennessee Wesleyan College in Athens tells the legend of Nocatula and her ill-fated lover, Conestoga. Stories remain of Nocatula's apparition haunting the campus in search of her true love. Just behind the sign, a recently placed sculpture represents the two legendary characters. *Photo by Stephanie Guy.*

Woods Memorial Hospital in Etowah has long been rumored to contain the ghost of a nurse. Former hospital employees claim sightings and swear that the stories are true. *Photo by Stephanie Guy.*

the hallway. The staff checks to see who the unidentified nurse is, but there is never anyone there. However, it is always noted that she is seen just before or right after a patient passes away. At other times, monitors and other medical equipment turn off or on, seemingly for no reason. Some nurses say that sometimes when they check on a patient, the person insists that another nurse had just left, even though no one else had been working in that area of the hospital. This specter, "Angelina," remains a topic of conversation among present and past staff members even today.

So many things can explain strange events: natural chemical reactions in marble, legends told from generation to generation, slow light switches and faulty electrical circuits, wind and, simply, our eyes playing tricks on us. But other things seem a bit harder to explain and leave us with only a ghost story of what we think happened, even if we don't really believe what we saw or felt. All stories are fibers of life that we hold to and share and, sometimes, add to in their telling and retelling, blurring facts and changing truth. Either way, whether of a legend or a mausoleum, in a school or even in the comforting form of a nurse, it is ultimately up to the listener to decide.

Old Steel, Cradles and Graves

As the sheets of steel façade began to come down under the workmen's careful hands, sparks flew from the torches cutting the support trusses on the old Cherokee Hardware building on the corner of Madison Avenue and Jackson Street in downtown Athens in 2006, revealing a storefront underneath that had not seen sunlight in more than fifty years. People passing through downtown noted old windows that had been filled in with concrete blocks and the dim remains of painted signs reading "Radios-Furniture-Pianos."

A few people still recall that Athens had names for its corners once, and this corner was known as the Henderson-Burn Corner. It was Lot 95 in the original plan of Athens, and records indicate that the first building that was built here was called Cleage Hall, constructed by Samuel Cleage, probably before 1840. It must have been a large, open building, as it was utilized for church services and county court at different times. When John M. Henderson purchased the building in 1872, it contained a store operated by McKeldin, Dement and Company, as well as the law office of the venerable attorney, chancellor and former Confederate supporter T.N. Van Dyke.

By 1888, records indicate that the building had burned down a few years before and was vacant, and as such it remained an eyesore for several years. In the later part of the century, the entire Madison Avenue Block was purchased by noted Athens attorney E.B. Madison, whose office was located two doors down.

In February 1897, two enterprising men (John W. Bayless and T.E. Moody) approached Madison and bought the property. By 1899, they had erected a brick store building on the site, much of which is believed to be within a portion of the original walls of Cleage Hall. During construction of the building, an error was made that caused the building to extend too far out into the city's right of way on Jackson Street by some fourteen inches. To remedy the problem, Bayless and Moody agreed to lease the fourteen-inch by seventy-nine-foot piece of land from the City of Athens for a period of ninety-nine years.

During the first one-third of the twentieth century, Bayless and Moody Hardware was a thriving business. It is said that a person could enter the store naked and come out with everything they could possibly need, including clothing, shoes, housewares, furniture, appliances and dishes. Eventually, Bayless and Moody expanded into the undertaking business and operated an embalming parlor and funeral home in the rear of the building. It is said that, since the business sold baby cribs, a sign on the side of the building

Located on the Athens Courthouse Square in the early years of the twentieth century, Bayless and Moody sold everything from baby rockers to coffins. *Courtesy of the McMinn County Historical Society.*

noted that it had everything from "Cradle to Grave." Advertisements for Bayless and Moody abound in old newspapers, and many photographs exist of the location. At some point, the post office even operated there, as the old safe still exists inside.

By 1941, both Bayless and Moody had passed away, and new owners took over the building and renamed it Cherokee Hardware Company. In an effort to modernize the look of the location, the windows were blocked over, and the steel façade was hung over the old brick storefront, giving way to the familiar look of Cherokee Hardware that most people remember. This business also thrived in its downtown location, although it also inherited the lease with the City of Athens of the fourteen-inch strip of ground. The city eventually quitclaimed the property to Cherokee Hardware in 1987, exercising the ninety-nine-year lease almost to the day. With the demise of Cherokee Hardware in the late 1990s, the building was subdivided into a fabric shop and an antiques store.

Some present owners seem to want to restore a bit of antiquity to the downtown area, and so at least a portion of the blue steel has come down to provide twenty-first-century citizens a look at a building that nineteenth-century citizens would recognize—sort of a time capsule that draws odd looks and questions from passersby, reminding us of some of our heritage and history, hidden under sheets and beams of steel from a time almost entirely forgotten.

The Grave Robbers

The caretaker of Cedar Grove Cemetery was making his rounds that cold winter morning in 1925, walking through the gravestones and planning his day of work, when he noticed something out of the ordinary. There, near the highest point of the cemetery, an old grave had been disturbed. It was a well-known grave, legendary even, of a supposed Cherokee leader who had died in the 1830s and had been buried in Athens. Upon closer inspection, he saw that the old grave had indeed been dug into, and with a chill up his spine that matched the cold of the January morning, he quickly left to summon the police.

Officers arrived as the sun rose higher in the sky, slowly burning away the early morning frost. It became clear that someone had dug a hole into the grave some four to five feet deep and the length of a casket; they had removed everything from the grave—the coffin, the body, everything. As the officers worked, Police Chief Welch also had to deal with a larger crowd of people who had come to see the crime scene. The only evidence left was two new picks and a short-handled shovel that apparently had been used to rob the grave, as well as a tin of common ladies' face makeup and a paper cone of the type used to hold thread. A trail of mud led from the open grave for about 150 feet to the nearest road, where tire tracks were found, along with what appeared to be a handle from the stolen casket.

Several old-timers appeared at the scene and talked among themselves about the crime and the history of the grave. One of the more outspoken was an aged Civil War veteran, A.M. Hacker, then in his eighty-first year. Mr. Hacker told the story that had been told to him by his father many years ago.

The grave had been that of a noted Cherokee who had been displaced by the whites moving into the area early in the state's history. As an old man, he had asked to be brought back to Athens to die and was subsequently buried at Cedar Grove Cemetery. Supposedly, the old Cherokee had requested

This grave in the Athens Cedar Grove Cemetery is believed to be that of Deerhorn, an old Cherokee who died during the Removal of 1836. On a cold winter night one hundred years later, Deerhorn's remains were again disturbed in a strange case of grave robbery. *Courtesy of the McMinn County Historical Society.*

to be buried in his robe with his head resting on a stone shaped like an arrowhead. Stones were placed over the grave, as was the fashion of earlier pioneer burials—mixing a Scotch-Irish tradition of stone cairns with the pioneer necessity of covering graves with stones to keep the wolves from disturbing the body. Mr. Hacker further related that his father had been one of the citizens involved in the burial.

Some fifteen years later, Mr. Hacker was interviewed regarding his status as one of the last surviving Civil War veterans in the area, and he again referred to a Cherokee grave at Cedar Grove and related the name of the Cherokee as "Deerhorn"—who had taken sick and died at a stagecoach house in Athens during the Indian Removal—and again stated that his father had assisted in the burial. All things considered, this may have been two stories about the same Cherokee.

As police officers spoke with Mr. Hacker and the other citizens as they investigated the crime, it became the consensus of those present that the probable reason the grave had been looted of its contents was an effort to steal some "buried treasure" that was rumored to have been in the grave.

This, too, was a common belief at the time and remains part of local legends today. No suspects were named, and it appears that the grave was refilled and left empty. The newspaper reported the crime as "Strangers Loot Old Indian's Tomb."

So it remains today, a strange-looking grave at Cedar Grove, covered in stones shaped like half-moons. Tales and legends grow like giant oaks over the years, and we wonder what really lies beneath the gravestones. Is the grave truly empty? Was the body ever found and returned? What was the real reason the thieves spent a cold night digging into an old man's grave? Whatever the answers are to these questions, and more, lies hidden there at Cedar Grove.

Haunted Williamsburg

The old house stands distinguished, one of the last remnants of a historic community known as both Williamsburg and Cantrell's Crossroads, along what was once a section of the Old Federal Road. The house has a rich history, built for John D. Williams during the years of 1858–60 by a man named McFarland. Bluegrass legend Roy Acuff once ate dinner here while running for governor. Senator Earnest Guffey married his wife, Carrie, in the library. Attorney Tom Taylor, who was Carrie's brother, told people that he kept a copperhead snake in a jar in his bedroom so his sisters would stay out. It has long been a source of stories, some historical and some haunted.

Tales abound about paranormal activity in the old house that could make one's hair stand up, like the one about the little girl on the tricycle with a bow in her hair, often visible in the front yard, who disappears before a second look, or stories of the wails of a slave chained in an upper bedroom, footsteps that seem to follow you up the stairs, mysterious lights in the library, a man heard clearing his throat, a baby heard crying, sounds of a person falling down the stairs and tales of some past resident hanging himself from the staircase. One past owner insisted that every time she went up the stairs, she felt a ghost pinch her.

Many people have experienced several of these occurrences, making one wonder why on earth its present owner, Doug Tullock, would want to live there.

"Because," laughs Doug, "a lot of the stories were just old tales that have been carried down through the years. Most of the things I've looked into, and I can explain them."

The J.D. Williams home, built in the mid-1800s, remains one of the Etowah area's most beautiful historic homes. Owner Doug Tullock has debunked most of the ghost stories surrounding the old house. *Photo by Stephanie Guy.*

Doug grew up familiar with the house. His father, English Tullock, once sharecropped for the Chestnut family, whose farm was just down the road. Doug purchased the Williams/Taylor House and surrounding property in the 1980s and has personally seen and heard a lot of the things that go bump in the night.

"I'll admit, stuff was a little weird at first," he says. "But I kept looking and listening, and found a logical explanation for a lot of it."

For example, there was the sound of footsteps following him up the stairs. After a little investigation into the stairs' construction, Doug had his answer.

"It's because the stairs are all tongue-and-groove. Over the years, the pieces of wood have grown a little loose due to humidity and wear, so when we step on the stair it causes the wood to move in the grooves. When you step off of it, a second or so later it moves back, and that is what you hear." And the pinching ghost? "Never had it happen to me," he says. "Maybe the other owner was prettier than I am."

As far as the unmistakable sound of a man clearing his throat, Doug figured that one out, too. "First of all, I noticed that it only happened when the wind blows. Turns out there is a loose piece of tin on the chimney that rattles and sounds like someone clearing their throat."

Then there are the mysterious lights that come on in the library. "Just a bad switch," says Doug.

Doug says that he has never seen or heard of the little girl on the tricycle, but he is familiar with some of the other stories. Still, he is unafraid of the stories surrounding his historic home. Although he's explained several of his paranormal issues away, he is the first to say that he can't explain them all: "I guess I will eventually be able to explain everything we see and hear, but there are still a few things I can't figure out. Like the music. Sometimes late at night, you can hear the faint sound of music, like classical music. We've looked all over the house, checked every radio and TV, but we can't find it… at least not yet."

Dead Man's Ticket

White Cliff, on the east summit of Starr Mountain near the junction of McMinn and Monroe Counties, is a popular site for hikers, history and legends. The White Cliff Springs Hotel once stood nearby, and the area was also the haunt of the hermit Mason Evans during the latter part of the nineteenth century. The hotel and hermit are long gone, but the cliffs remain and offer beautiful views of the Rural Vale community and the Tellico Mountains in the distance.

The one-hundred-foot cliffs are also very dangerous, and several lives have been lost there. The story of one such death stands out, related to me some time ago by Athens resident Buddy Biddle. Buddy's great-grandfather was Tom Evans, the first proprietor of the Evans Funeral Home in Athens. It seems that in the late 1800s, a young man from the Midwest rode a train to Athens and took a carriage to Starr Mountain to visit his sweetheart at White Cliff Springs Hotel. It was popular in those days, as it remains today, for couples to take walks along the nearby cliffs. As young men often do, the young man was acting a bit recklessly on the cliffs when he slipped and fell to his death in the presence of his girlfriend. Men from the hotel climbed down, recovered the young man's broken body and brought it back to the hotel.

Mr. Evans was called. He traveled from Athens up to the mountain, where he cleaned the body and embalmed it at the hotel. He had to, for the body

White Cliff Springs Hotel, on the summit of Starr Mountain, was the scene of countless local stories, not the least of which concerned the death of a young man on the nearby cliffs. *Author's collection.*

would begin to putrefy before he could get it back to Athens in his wagon, and it would not be in a good condition to send back home, which was the wish of the young man's family. Once the body was embalmed, Evans dressed it, placed it in a new coffin and transported it back to Athens.

Mr. Evans was not too concerned about getting the body back to the Midwest. In the young man's belongings, Evans had found that the deceased had bought a two-way railroad ticket, and Mr. Evans had the ticket in hand when he took the coffin to the depot on White Street.

But the railroad clerk refused to honor the ticket. "Absolutely not," said the clerk flatly. "That ticket is for a passenger seat, sir. The coffin must be placed in the baggage car, and that will cost you $100."

Mr. Evans remained firm. "But this man bought a two-way ticket. His passage back home is already paid for. I insist that you honor the return ticket." Still, no matter how hard Mr. Evans pleaded, the clerk refused. "That is a seat ticket. Baggage will cost you $100."

"Fine, then," growled Mr. Evans. "If you insist, you leave me no choice. If it is a seat he purchased, then so be it. I shall remove the body from the coffin and place the dead man in the seat he paid for."

The clerk grew wide-eyed with disbelief, snatched the return ticket out of Mr. Evans's hand and stamped it as approved. The coffin was placed in the baggage car, and the dead man enjoyed the use of his return ticket, although in the baggage car rather than the passenger compartment.

Houses of the Dead

In certain cemeteries, among the stones, they sit quietly over a grave, odd and seemingly out of place; they are buildings over the graves—houses of the dead, if you will. They are known by many names, such as spirit houses, grave shelters or board mausoleums. But most are referred to as "grave houses" and, although rare, can still be found in many areas across the Southeast, including East Tennessee. Grave houses are "supra-burial constructions," meaning that they are "constructed over the grave." Grave houses are not mausoleums, nor are they crypts, but rather are covered shelters built over a below-ground burial.

The trail to researching the history of this tradition immediately forks and then forks again and again. There is evidence that the tradition originated in Germany, as well as other evidence that it came from the "box and table" grave coverings in England. Still other resources insist that it is a derivative of certain Native American burial practices. So it is really difficult to determine exactly where the tradition came from—most likely it is a combination of some or all of these traditions.

There is no doubt about the purpose of a grave house, however, and that is to protect a grave from the elements or from other threats. Placing a roofed structure over a grave will certainly protect it from sunlight, rain, sleet and snow. And when enclosed by walls or wired sides, no animals, livestock or people can damage the grave, either. Some grave houses are large enough for visitors to enter, allowing for grieving family members to sit and spend time at a grave in any type of weather.

No specific pattern of design or construction is required for grave houses. They may be just large enough to cover a single grave or large enough to cover several burials. Roofs may be flat or pitched and covered in shingles or tin. The sides may be entirely closed in with wood siding or be built of solid brick with a locking door; some even have windows installed. Others have open sides covered in boards with spaces in between, with latticework or with wire fencing.

Some grave houses are true "houses," such as this brick structure that is built over the graves of the Plank family at Short Creek Cemetery. *Photo by Stephanie Guy.*

I had seen grave houses but had not realized their uniqueness until I read about the work done by John and Retta Waggoner of Smith County, Tennessee. After several years of genealogy and grave site documentation, the Waggoners began photographing and listing grave houses on their website (www.thegravewalkers/gravehousesdirectory.com). So far, they have photographed and listed grave houses all across Tennessee, as well as many in Alabama, Georgia, Kentucky, Mississippi, South Carolina and Louisiana. One look at their collection and I was hooked.

Some Southeast Tennessee counties such as Bradley, Rhea and McMinn include sites the Waggoners have located. The Sugar Creek Cemetery in Bradley County is the home of an old brick grave house with a shingled roof and steel door that covers the graves of Leander and Mary Hughes, who died in 1868 and 1876, respectively. Two cemeteries in Rhea County have grave houses. A white wood house trimmed in green with a tin roof, similar to a small barn, stands in the Hurst Cemetery. It holds four graves, with two of the markers still readable over the graves of W.H. Smith and Birdie Rogers, who both passed in 1945. In the Johnson-Stand Cemetery is a well-kept white pole/barn-type structure with a green tin roof. The inviting grave house has open sides enclosed with white picket fencing and protects the graves of Bill (1998) and Arkie Cox (1975).

In McMinn County, at Short Creek Baptist Church Cemetery, are not one but three grave houses. One is a white-trimmed shed with a tin roof and open sides covered with wire and decorated with landscaping, mulched plants and a bench. Here lie the graves of William Peyton (1955), John W. (1928) and Lartie Allen Whiteside (1962). Not far away is an imposing brick grave house with a plaque that reads: "This building erected around the Plank family graves by Lawrence Carter as per request by the will of WH Plank Apr 1967, Rev. J. McCleary, Builder." Inside are the graves of William H. Plank (1963), Amanda Reed Plank (1914) and a Plank infant (1914). Last is the small, white, wood-latticed grave house of little three-year-old Luther Reed, who died in 1901. The tiny grave house has a concrete base and a shingled roof.

As a deputy sheriff patrolling the Short Creek Church several years ago, I often drove through the Short Creek Cemetery, checking for vandals or trespassers. On moonless nights, my patrol car spotlight often lit up the grave houses, and not understanding what I was seeing, I must say that it was a little

This grave house at Short Creek Cemetery in McMinn County is one of few such structures in Southeast Tennessee. *Photo by Stephanie Guy.*

creepy. But thanks to people like John and Retta Waggoner, I have learned that they are remnants of long-lost traditions, still maintained to remind us of the special care that loved ones sometimes exhibit at a grave site, intending on marking the resting place with not just a stone but a house—to cover it, protect it and make it a special and unique place.

THE DEAD AND THE ALMOST DEAD

Sigmund Freud once said, "The goal of all life is death." The end of life and earthly existence plagues every human and touches every person in all places. Every person attends a funeral service for someone they knew or loved in order to pay their last respects and mourn the death of another person. The funeral service is a long-standing tradition that is observed in many different ways across the world. In most places in America, the funeral home has become the most popular location for a family to conduct this ceremony, but being in the business of death is not for everyone. It takes a special kind of person to work in the funeral home business.

Many years ago, funeral "parlors" existed in some towns and provided a place where the dead person could be properly prepared for burial and embalmed and where a coffin was made for the specific body to be laid to rest. But in rural areas, transporting a decomposing and unembalmed body was impractical, and it was up to the family and neighbors to perform the work.

A part of the funeral then involved the family and neighbors "sitting up with the dead" overnight. It was a tradition that was based on the notion that if the deceased person did not wake up during the night, they must certainly be dead and could be buried the next day. A fear of burying someone alive once persisted and spawned this tradition.

Stories abound from those old days that are both morose and humorous, when medical science had not yet reached the point of properly determining if a person was truly dead. The fear of burying someone alive was based on stories like that of the woman whose grave was opened several months after her burial in order for her grieving husband to retrieve a cherished ring from her finger. To the horror of the family, the dead woman's body and face were found to be contorted grotesquely, and the underside of the coffin lid was clawed and scratched by the poor woman, who had been accidentally buried alive. A similar story involved a woman who died after giving birth to a stillborn baby. Both the mother and baby were buried together, and a few

"Uncle" Joe Elliott stands behind the tiny coffin holding the body of his deceased grandchild. The old man's grief is evident in this poignant photograph, taken in the 1930s at Old Liberty Hill Cemetery—one last image preserved of the child before being placed beneath the red, sandy soil. Photographs of the deceased were not uncommon years ago, when family members were unable to travel to view the body at the funeral. *Author's collection.*

nights later, a man reported hearing noises from the grave that sounded like a baby crying. Neighbors quickly dug down and opened the coffin to find the baby alive.

My grandfather, the late Winston Guy, was both a longtime police officer and an employee at Bordwine Funeral Home in Etowah. He told me stories that he had heard or knew of from years past in the funeral home business.

He said once that an old man had died and that his elderly wife called the funeral home to pick up the body. The dead man was taken to the funeral home and placed on the embalming table under a sheet. It was late at night, and a young employee leaned back in a chair by the table to catch a quick nap before the embalmer arrived. But the old man was not dead—he'd only had a mild stroke. He awoke under the sheet and, still disoriented, reached over and grabbed the young man by the shoulder. The embalmer was just coming in the door as the screaming young employee burst outside, white as a sheet and running for his life.

The late Jerry Clower recounted a similar story in which a body was picked up at a morgue, and while the hearse driver was inside, a hitchhiker approached the morgue attendant and asked if he could catch a ride in the back beside the body. The attendant shrugged and said that he guessed it would be all right. But somehow, the morgue attendant forgot to tell the hearse driver that he had an extra passenger. As the hearse drifted silently down the highway at fifty miles an hour through the dark night, the hitchhiker reached through the curtain and, tapping the driver's shoulder, said, "You mind if I smoke back here?" The driver never touched the brake. He just opened the door and "got out" of the hearse onto the highway. Luckily, no one was severely injured.

My grandfather also told of a long-ago wake being held in the home of an old man who was severely bent with arthritis, to the point that straps were placed under the man's clothes to hold his upper body down into the coffin. With family and friends sitting up talking quietly late in the night, one of the house cats got into the coffin. Stretching its claws, as cats are wont to do, it caused one of the straps to break, and the old man "rose up" in front of everyone. The mourners also rose up—they left no funeral home chair or fan undisturbed as they tore their way out of the house, trying to outrun at least the slowest of the group in getting away from the old man before he had completely exited his coffin.

Part V

Politics, Small Towns and Giant People

The actions of people make our history come alive, and in the retelling of these stories, I like to think that I am resurrecting the dead for a little while, allowing them to breathe and move and live in the reader's imagination. Sometimes, ordinary people can be downright heroic when faced with the right circumstances, and I hope you enjoy the inspiration of these few tidbits.

Etowah's Doughboys

It was 1918, and the Great War was winding down in Europe. A great amount of patriotism was sweeping over America, and A.B. Bayless, superintendent of the Atlanta Division of the L&N Railroad, was caught up in the fervor.

Looking out of his office window at the grassy lawn of the L&N Depot in Etowah, Bayless envisioned a monument to the veterans of the war the likes of which had never been done in the burgeoning railroad town. His idea was to honor not just soldiers and sailors from Etowah but also those from the entire McMinn County Third Civil District. A committee was formed called the World War Soldiers and Sailors Memorial Association.

The Etowah area had a lot to be proud of concerning the soldiers it sent into the war. In 1910, a company of national guardsmen was organized in Etowah by R.W. Green, known as Company A, Third Tennessee Infantry,

The 117th Infantry was made up of McMinn County men, mostly from the Etowah area. Soon after assisting in the capture of Pancho Villa, the men were called to service during World War I, earning them many heroic laurels. *Courtesy of the McMinn County Historical Society.*

and later as Company L. An armory was located on the west side of Ohio Avenue near Ninth Street. About 1912, Captain D.W. Lillard became commanding officer. In 1916, the company saw its first real duty when it was sent to assist in the capture of Pancho Villa on the Texas-Mexico border. By the time the company returned home in March 1917, the war in Europe had escalated to the point that in June it was again called into federal service. After some training at Camp Sevier, South Carolina, the boys from Etowah sailed for Europe on May 11, 1918.

The days of May 23–24 were spent in England, and then the boys crossed over into France and began making their way to the front. Company L served with the British Third and Fourth Armies in Belgium, Ypres-Lys and in the Somme Offensive. They were also involved in the Allies' breaking of the Hindenburg Line on September 29. Brought out for rest, the company was at Heilly when the armistice was signed. As the American forces withdrew over the next several months, the men of Company L returned to the United States and were mustered out of service at Chickamauga Park in April 1919.

One officer, Lieutenant William Eckel, and forty-five enlisted men were killed in action. Two officers, Captain Lillard and Lieutenant Charles

This monument was placed on the lawn of the Etowah Depot soon after the 117th's return from the "War to End All Wars," honoring the local men who had served so heroically. *Photo by Stephanie Guy.*

Walters, were wounded, along with ninety-four enlisted men. The company was awarded one Medal of Honor and sixteen Distinguished Service Crosses, along with many British and French military honors.

The highly decorated men returned to Etowah to their heroes' welcome, and the company returned to its status as a National Guard unit. Soon, it was reorganized as Company G, 117th Infantry, and was provided a new armory in an old livery stable on Eighth Street, where KC's Supermarket would later be located.

With the fervor present to honor their soldiers, the monument organization raised $3,500 and was able to obtain a thirty-foot circle of ground in front of the depot on Tennessee Avenue. There a monument was built of Georgia marble for $3,000, with the remaining funds being used to construct walkways and landscaping around the little park. It was dedicated on May 30, 1922, with Brigadier General Cary Spence as program speaker. In 1931, with approval from the L&N Railroad, the park was expanded to include a "modern" bandstand built of twenty-seven tons of flagstone from Crossville, Tennessee. The stone, wiring and labor were all donated by Etowah residents and businesses.

The monument and bandstand remain today as symbols of Etowah's early growth and its important contribution to national and world affairs. The monument reads, in part, "To our living dead—that company of shining souls who gave their youth that the world might grow old in peace."

ONE STREET CORNER, A THOUSAND STORIES

Crossroads have long been points of interest, providing the traveler with a place to take a new direction. Whether it be an intersection of rural roads or a city street corner, a place where paths cross causes people to interact, and when people interact, stories are born. What stories can one city corner tell? The southeast corner of the public square in Athens has a long history, involving bricks, hotels, the Trail of Tears, U.S. presidents, stagecoaches, giant hailstones and even a little prostitution.

When the town of Athens was laid out in 1821, this corner was noted as Lot 94. The first known building constructed here, about 1830, was the Athens Hotel (also later known as the Bridges Hotel). This hotel was a two-story brick structure built by Cleage and Crutchfield, the itinerant contractors who are responsible for many fine homes and public buildings from Botetourt County, Virginia, to Chattanooga, Tennessee. The building was built with bricks hand-made by Cleage's Angolan slaves, who themselves were master brick makers.

The building served as a hotel, as well as the stagecoach stop, for Athens. The main north–south road through McMinn County passed over what is now Madison Avenue, connecting a route from the Cherokee Nation south of the Hiwassee to all points north, including Knoxville, Washington and New York.

In 1836–37, the hotel was the headquarters of General John Ellis Wool, who was charged with the difficult task of rounding up Cherokees who had not yet migrated to lands west of the Mississippi. Wool's stay in Athens is well documented, as his troops camped just across Eastanaulee Creek, just past the present Jackson Street Bridge. Wool sympathized with the Cherokees, and after he intervened on their behalf against some illegal actions in Alabama, he was relieved of his command.

Before the railroad was operational in 1854, the hotel was the resting point of many notable people who visited Athens, including General Winfield Scott and presidential candidates Henry Clay, Andrew Jackson and James K. Polk; it has also long been rumored that David Crockett stayed there during his term as a congressman. When the Civil War came to McMinn County, and General William T. Sherman needed a place to stay as he operated here in 1864, it was the Bridges Hotel that he chose for his headquarters, while his officers stayed at the Van Dyke House.

The hotel remained a place of business under several owners until it was demolished in 1825 to make way for a new hotel, known as the

The Athens/Bridges Hotel is pictured here. Built in 1834, the hotel was known by many names. It was the most commonly used place of lodging, as the Athens stagecoach stop was here. *Courtesy of the McMinn County Historical Society.*

Robert E. Lee, which was opened in 1926. The Robert E. Lee offered patrons modern rooms, with a well-stocked food shop in the lobby. Again, Henderson Corner was a central point of travel, as the bus station that operated from across the street provided a steady stream of patrons. Locals would gather in the lobby and on benches outside to converse and do business. Several businesses were operated in the front of the hotel from time to time, including that of Bullet Boyer.

It was on this corner in 1932 where, after a severe hailstorm, a huge twelve-pound hailstone was found. It drew a great amount of attention and was even mentioned in newspapers as far away as New York. Sometime later, the "hailstone" was found to be nothing more than a prank pulled by Bullet Boyer and his fun-loving employee Howard Baless.

When the Highway 11 bypass was built in the late 1940s, and highway traffic began to be drawn away from the downtown area, the Robert E. Lee fell on hard times. By the late 1960s and early 1970s, the rooms were rented out to persons of less-than-reputable character, some of whom were ladies who applied themselves to the "oldest profession" and unfortunately tainted the reputation of the old hotel until the City of Athens cleaned out such behavior.

The building has changed ownership over the past few decades, having been used as an apartment building and, at other times, remaining vacant. Today, the Robert E. Lee building is home to a restaurant providing fine dining to area residents. It remains a focal point downtown, sitting on a single small street corner piled high with stories and history.

"Going to the Store" in Early Etowah

When the town of Etowah was literally carved out of a collection of farms and swamps by the L&N Railroad in 1906, people immediately began moving into the boomtown. Avenues were laid off from north to south and named for states, beginning with Tennessee Avenue, and streets were run east to west and numbered from First to Tenth. Most lots were sold for homes west of Tennessee Avenue, with most of the main street lots reserved for businesses.

No town can survive without a retail and service industry, and stores immediately began to spring up along Etowah's dusty thoroughfare. Most, if not all, were wood-frame buildings in the beginning, with merchants providing the necessary items to complete the daily life of the turn-of-the-century family. Much was needed, as more people came on a daily basis, looking for new homes, new opportunities, new jobs and a better life, which the railroad town was sure to offer.

The first edition of the *Etowah Enterprise* on December 5, 1907, gives a glimpse of the first stores in town through its advertisements. In his ad, general store owner O.L. Davis proudly stated that his was the first store to open in Etowah. He would soon be followed in business by John Rains and the McKinney brothers. Davis dealt in general merchandise and is recorded to have located on the corner of Seventh and Tennessee, where the Etowah Arts Commission now resides. On the corner of Ninth and Ohio was the general store owned by R.L. Cunningham.

The first post office was operated out of John Rains's general store, little more than a "shanty" near the freight depot. J.H. Stafford advertised "drygoods and notion, clothing, shoes, hats, gent's furnishings, and a complete line of hardware." Stafford would later operate a hotel in town.

The McKinney brothers at the corner of Tennessee and Sixth carried groceries along with dry goods, notions, shoes and hats. J.F. Wagner on Tennessee Avenue sold a line of "staple and fancy groceries," as well as fresh

Etowah grew from a muddy farm to a bustling modern railroad boomtown in only a few years. It rivaled the county seat of Athens eight miles to the west, a rivalry that still exists today that transcends McMinn County sports and politics. *Courtesy of Durant Tullock.*

and salted meats. Wagner also bottled soft drinks at Imperial Bottling Works. The Hedden brothers sold furniture from their store near the depot, as did Sterchi Brothers & Tillery located on Ninth Street.

Other stores included Griffin's, Reed's and W.J. Sample's, all on Ninth Street between Tennessee and Ohio, along with Fronenberger's at Ninth and Tennessee and H.D. Rule and Company next door. P.A. Kinser operated the first drugstore nearby, where Rule Furniture later stood. Additional businesses included Cunningham and Watts Livery Stable on the corner of Eighth and Pennsylvania, where the remains of an old service station sit today. A.J. Haynes ran a lumberyard, which was no doubt kept busy with the growth of the new town. A clothing store run by J.N. Lewis was opened in the spring of 1907 and was a popular location to purchase men's and women's apparel.

Times would pass, and with the coming of the automobile, new businesses emerged in the form of tire stores and service stations; livery stables, blacksmiths and harness shops began to disappear. Other businesses closed for numerous reasons, including death, competition and buyouts. By 1950, only three of Etowah's original businesses remained: O.L. Reed of Reed Brothers, J.N. Lewis and Griffin's. Griffin's was the only store to remain in its original location on Ninth Street, outlasting all of the others until it closed in the 1970s. Coincidentally, I am fortunate to own two of the store counters from Griffin's. Huge and heavy beaded-board things, one sits as a centerpiece in my family's great room.

Sometimes, late at night, I swear I can hear the *clink* of an old cash register coming from the great room, along with what sounds to be groceries being placed in a paper "poke." Strangely enough, I find that things fall off the old counter a lot. Maybe it's Mr. Griffin or his daughter, Maggie, still trying to move some merchandise.

The Athens Academy

In the years after the Civil War, with a huge number of newly freed blacks in the South, several northern organizations began financing education and opportunities for this underserved segment of the population. The United Presbyterian Church took special note of the educational and spiritual needs of this newly free population through its "Freedman of the South" board. The concerned Yankee Presbyterians rightly believed that a good community was founded on education and morality.

Like many other communities, McMinn County benefited from the Presbyterians' work. In 1892, a beautiful new Presbyterian church was built in Athens on White Street, with two towers and opera seating that rivaled most white church buildings. Also, a school was founded by the Presbyterians called the Athens Academy.

The academy stood near the present Laycock-Hobbs Funeral Home, and it was a two-story frame building with a bell tower. It had five classrooms and a thirty- by fifty-foot auditorium. The school was funded almost entirely by the Presbyterians, both in construction and operation in addition to its teachers. Even tuition money and clothing could be provided for students who were in need. A newspaper article from 1901 reported that the academy accepted both local students and also those from other areas—it "has its doors open to students from a distance. It places an education within the reach of young people of limited means." The school was closely associated with the new church across the street and was "thoroughly and earnestly Christian." The article went on to note that "the prospects for the future of the Academy are good. The school is gaining many friends among the citizens of both races. The moral and religious training which are being taught by the teachers are being seen in the homes of the older people, and in the daily life and character of the youth."

The instructors were from all over, including Athens. John T. Arter, principal, was a graduate of Knoxville College and Allegheny Theological

Founded by the Presbyterian Church in 1892, the Athens Academy was one of the premier black schools in the South, staffed with instructors from all across the world. *Courtesy of the McMinn County Historical Society.*

Seminary and also was minister of the new Presbyterian church. His wife, Minnie, was a Knoxville College alumna who had taught for many years in her hometown of Americus, Georgia. Professor G.T. Collier was an experienced teacher from North Carolina and was assisted by his wife, Louise, a graduate of Atlanta University. Assistant Principal James W. Fisher was also a Knoxville College graduate and an experienced teacher. Miss Christianita Totten was of the Danish West Indies, had graduated from Knoxville College and was a veteran teacher from the Knoxville schools. Miss Lea Jones came from Texas. Henry W. Cleage was from Athens. Cleage had attended school under J.L. Cook, who with Presbyterian assistance had actually founded the original academy in a three-room building in 1892. Cleage, like most of the faculty, had attended Knoxville College and had returned home to teach. He married one of the students, a pretty young girl named Minnie, who also stayed on for a while to assist her husband.

The black community had several other local men of note who were associated with the school, such as Hugh Keith, George McKeldin, Will

Keith, J.D. Logan, P.D. Keith and Richard Brannon. Hugh Keith was supervisor of the mail and transfer business in Athens. P.D. Keith owned a large farm in addition to a draying and livery business. Richard Brannon was a successful businessman, owned a considerable amount of property and served for more than ten years as an Athens alderman.

For the next quarter century, the school continued to successfully educate local black students from all across the region until 1925, when the Athens Academy was destroyed by fire. Classes continued to be held in the United Presbyterian Church until a new school was built with funding from McMinn County, the City of Athens and the Rosenwald Fund; it was opened on December 10, 1926. The name was changed to the J.L. Cook School to honor the original founder. Even in the era of Jim Crow laws and the nonsense of "separate but equal" facilities, Cook School became one of the premier schools in the South until its closing due to desegregation in 1966.

During the years of desegregation and civil rights that were marred with violence and social turmoil, fewer problems existed in McMinn County compared to many other locations in Tennessee and across the South. This was due in no small part to the Athens Academy and, later, the Cook School, both of which set in place a proud legacy of black education and leadership in McMinn County.

Indians, Senators and Governors: The Forest Hill Academy

The men came riding up to Forest Hill Academy that day in 1837, calling to the headmaster of the school, Professor Charles P. Samuels. There were Indians coming, the men said—a large group marching into Athens. Soldiers had been in the area rounding up Cherokees for removal to the West, and the Indians might be gathering together in revolt for an assault on the town. The riders advised Professor Samuels and the other men present to arm themselves and be ready for an attack and then rode off toward Athens some two miles west. Mrs. Samuels nervously gathered her young sons around the hearth in the parlor of their home in the academy. She told them to kneel down and pray, which they did, but no Indian attack ever came. Still, it made a deep impression on the Samuels boys.

Soon afterward, two influential Cherokees arrived at the school along with their young sons. The Indian boys were dressed in clothes matching

Professor Charles P. Samuels, in a portrait that hangs in the McMinn County Living Heritage Museum. Samuels took over Forest Hill Academy in 1830 and remained headmaster until his death, educating many young white and Cherokee students who would later factor into Tennessee history. *Courtesy of the McMinn County Living Heritage Museum.*

most any of the white schoolchildren, and both of their fathers stood nearby neatly dressed in coats, ties and breeches. One of the fathers, John Ross, was light-skinned and did not even speak the Indian language. His sons, John and Charlie, were also light-skinned and stood waiting nearby. The other man, Jack Walker, was darker and wore a silver ring in his nose. His two sons, Tom and Jack, waited with the Ross boys while their fathers spoke to Professor Samuels about the Indian Removal, which neither Ross nor Walker believed would be totally enforced. Both men were racially mixed and wanted their Cherokee sons to be enrolled in a white school. Forest Hill Academy, located near a big spring by the banks of Eastanaulee Creek, both was a good school and was located close to the Cherokee Nation south of the Hiwassee River. After some talk, it was agreed that the Cherokee boys could board at the school, although under one condition: Jack Walker must cut off his long, coarse hair.

At first, the boy objected. However, when the elder Walker threatened to leave Tom at the school and take Jack Jr. home, the boy relented. Later, when it was told to Professor Samuels's son, Charles, that he would have to sleep in the same bed as Jack Walker, young Samuels worried that Jack would scalp him. Not to worry, his mother said—half-breeds aren't prone to scalping.

During their year at the school, the Walker and Ross boys excelled in their studies and became fast friends with the Samuels boys. John Ross and Jack Walker were leaders of the Cherokees and were impressed with Professor Samuels's efforts. In 1838, Ross and Walker both left for the Cherokee reservation in Oklahoma, and their sons followed soon after, leaving their school friends behind. Ross later wrote to the professor in an effort to entice him to come and start a school in Oklahoma, but Mrs. Samuels refused to leave.

The Samuels family remained in charge of the school from 1830 to 1850, enjoying the tutelage of many boys who later became distinguished men, with the family names of Cook, Lowery, Cleage, Crutchfield, Bridges, Slover, Brown, Morgan, Reynolds, Crawford, Jackson, Ballew, Matthews, Jarnigan, Reed, McGaughey and more. Among them in adulthood would be numbered a governor of Missouri, a U.S. senator, two governors of Tennessee, a chief justice of the State of Alabama, some congressmen and several judges.

Reverend Seth Church took over as headmaster in 1850 and was succeeded by Reverend George Caldwell in 1852 after Church's death. On February 17, 1853, the academy was completely destroyed by a fire that began in the frame portion and consumed the brick structure. The following month, the school's trustees solicited builders to construct a new two-story brick academy building closer to Athens, and a hill on College Street was selected for the site. On August 25, 1854, the building was in a "rapid state of construction." In October 1854, though the "brick, mortar, and woodwork" were completed, the building was still unoccupied. The academy was reopened on January 8, 1855, with Mr. A.C. Carnes as headmaster of fifty pupils.

In 1856, the building sustained some damage, possibly from a windstorm, and Forest Hill was not reopened until April 1857 under John Gierlow of Macon, Georgia. Others who headed the academy were Dudley Evans (1861), A.A. Newman (1862), Mr. Eblin (1869) and many others. Like many town buildings during the Civil War, Forest Hill was used to house sick and wounded soldiers.

In 1881, J.F. McCarron arrived to take over the school. McCarron was also successful as schoolmaster, teaching the children to sing multiplication tables and instructing them in astronomy, for it was said that McCarron was "as familiar with the stars as with his next door neighbors." Ms. Laura Dodson assisted him as instructor. Later, McCarron would take over the Athenian newspaper and enjoy a distinguished career as publisher.

The long and distinguished history of Forest Hill Academy came to an end in 1903 when the City of Athens reorganized its school system and the building became a city school. It was operated until 1906, when a larger building was built a few blocks to the north, known as "Forest Hill School," which operated until 1971. Few today know the school's story and its significance in local, state and national history of the educational beginnings of so many notable figures.

The Underdogs: Cook High's 1933 Basketball Team

The old Cook High School turned out many great athletes while it was in operation, even though the equipment, courts and fields were not up to par with most white schools in East Tennessee. Oftentimes, the equipment was used and damaged, and at times basketball players had to share shoes during games. But whether in baseball, football or basketball, athletes from J.L. Cook were determined to compete.

One sports team that stood out was the 1933 Cook basketball team, made up of Melvin Matlock, Sewell Ward, William Queener, Ulyses Queener, Ed Cansler, Ump Cansler, Henry Moss and James Cates. Cook High had only been operating for seven years and was still building its athletic teams. Having a fair season, the team traveled to Nashville to participate in the black high school state tournament. Professor W.E. Nash was one of the faculty members who coached and traveled with the team to the competition. Nash was never one to avoid a challenge when it came to his students.

According to Nash, they arrived in Nashville at about one o'clock in the afternoon on the day of the tournament and found that their first game would be with top-seeded Booker T. Washington High School from Memphis. Booker T. was a forty-year-old institution with the best basketball team in the state. It seemed clear that the tournament officials intended on eliminating the lesser-ranked Cook High early in the contest.

Professor W.E. Nash served as teacher and principal of Cook School for many years. He coached the 1933 basketball team that played for the state title only to be denied due to a single ragged shoe. Nash was a longtime resident of Athens, passing away at the age of 106. He is pictured here with his wife. *Courtesy of the McMinn County Living Heritage Museum.*

That evening, the Cook players expressed a desire to have some good bologna for their pregame meal. Professor Nash, uncertain if this would be good food before a game, sought the advice of Kingsport's Coach Dobbins, who said, "No bologna." But when Nash told Dobbins who Cook would be playing, Dobbins retracted his statement. "Give them anything they want," he said, "because you all don't have a chance." Nash went ahead and got the boys some bologna, and at 8:00 p.m. it was game time.

When the Cook High team took the court with secondhand uniforms and worn-out shoes, there was almost a dead silence. The entire team consisted of eight players, and few if any fans had been able to travel from Athens to the game. Then came the Booker T. team, twenty-five players strong, and the stands erupted into a terrific cheer. The Cook team assembled for a brief talk from Nash, and with the tipoff, the game was underway.

Booker T. hit the first basket, and again the crowd cheered, followed by a basket by Cook, for which hardly any noise was made. It went on like this, back and forth down the court. But then a change began to take place in the crowd. Although they were the underdogs, playing the best team in the state, the Cook team matched Booker T. point for point, playing outstanding basketball. As the game played on, cheers began to erupt every time Cook scored. It was small at first, but as it became clear that Cook had come to play, the fans began to cheer wildly for Cook. When it was over, Cook had won, defeating the number one team.

Advancing further into the tournament, Cook beat Centerville and then Coach Dobbins's Kingsport team to advance to the championship game with Lebanon High. For four quarters, the teams were in a dead heat. But in the fourth, William Queener's shoe blew out, and he had to go to the bench, hopeful in finding a teammate with the same-sized foot. But while he was out, Lebanon scored twice, and time ran out on the Cook High team.

When the tournament awards were handed out afterward, forward James Cate won the top scorer award and was selected all-state and all-southern.

It is as sad today as it was in 1933 that a single shoe would decide a state high school basketball championship, and the memory of the Cook High School team has almost drifted away with the passing of those eight determined athletes, who with worn-out shoes showed the state that it took heart, not uniforms, to be competitors.

Miss Myrtle

Miss Myrtle Webb bounced over miles and miles of rutted dirt roads, first in a horse-drawn carriage and then in a Model T Ford and, still later, a DeSoto. She traveled through nearly every McMinn County community she could, going from house to house to offer her services. She always spoke with the woman, the wife or the mother. She made observations of the family's quality of life, how clean the yard and house were, if there was a garden spot and if there were some livestock, and she also offered helpful suggestions.

"I can show you some things," she would say, "things you can do to make your life better, and maybe even make you some extra money."

Sometimes, her offer was refused. "This is the way we live, and we're happy with it," some of the women would say. But most were curious, especially when it came to the possibility of making some extra money.

Oftentimes, a neighbor would be called over, and Myrtle would talk to both women at the same time. She gave them books and brochures, if they could read. But always she demonstrated—showed them how to clean and

Ms. Myrtle Webb spent many years as a "home demonstration agent" in East Tennessee, teaching rural women the skills to market their own artwork, produce, weaving and other homemade items. *Courtesy of the McMinn County Historical Society.*

how to take a little paint and spruce things up a bit. "You have to know how to cook and sew," she would say in her shy way. And when she talked about making money, many times she started with chickens. Chickens were cheap and easy to care for, and they laid eggs. Extra eggs could be sold, and people would trade things for them. If the poor farm wife was already marketing her eggs to local neighbors, then Myrtle would smile through her round glasses and make other suggestions.

They could plant flowers and learn to arrange and sell them. They could learn to make little gardens for their families and sell the extra produce, use a sewing machine to make and repair clothing, bake or can goods. If the family had a milk cow, she told them where they could sell their freshly churned cream and butter. A woman could provide for her family and make money, Myrtle said with her toothy grin, brushing back her unruly brown hair. She can earn her own money for things for her family and things for herself. It was a novel idea, a rural woman making things and making her own money. In the 1920s, a little money could go a long way, especially for a poor farm woman.

Myrtle would stay as long as necessary—answering questions and making suggestions—doing her job as the county home demonstration agent, part of a national project to improve the lives of rural families during the first half of the twentieth century. The project focused on an underused resource: hungry, hardworking rural wives with time on their hands and a desire to better themselves. Every year, she petitioned the McMinn County court to give her additional funds to operate and buy the supplies she needed to get the women started. Sometimes she taught groups of women things like how to make a cotton mattress, rather than straw or feather ticks; after sleeping on the cotton, people said they thought they had "died and gone to heaven." She organized ladies into "Home Demonstration Clubs" so that their skills could be practiced and passed on. Other times, she coordinated sessions presented by instructors from the University of Tennessee. Not only were the women learning and doing, they were also meeting one another and growing out of the old expectations of a rural farm wife (only cooking, cleaning, having babies and hauling wood).

When the Great Depression came, Myrtle was both an educator and a savior. She taught families the skills they could use to get by and survive: how to grow their own food, make and mend their own clothing and other necessities, repair things, reuse and recycle items so as not to waste anything and get what they could spare off the farm and to market for a small profit.

With the coming of the Tennessee Valley Authority and electricity, Myrtle adapted her demonstrations so as to include advice on cooking with an electric stove and how to use a refrigerator or an electric iron. County demonstration agents like Myrtle organized community markets at which the women would gather and offer their products for sale, a "Women's Farm Market." People came to buy and trade, and wives were able to provide additional income to their families. Homes and lives improved, and all the while there was Myrtle, from 1919 until 1954, traveling over every hill, through every valley and along every road in the county, teaching, demonstrating and encouraging. By the time she retired, after thirty-five years of work, she had driven more than 280,000 miles and improved the lives of thousands of men, women and children. She had nurtured and established 4-H clubs for children; for the adults, twenty-three Home Demonstration Clubs were meeting in McMinn County. Her outstanding work was met with high honors from the State of Tennessee and the National Home Demonstration Agent's Association.

She never married, and she lived in her later years with a niece in Knoxville. She died in May 1980 and was buried in Newport, but her work in McMinn County—with her easy smile and her glasses dusty from the roads—should not be forgotten. Miss Myrtle Webb's dedication allowed her to personally change people's lives for the better, and she remains one of those special people whose quiet work made McMinn County what it is today.

THE CAMPBELL–VAN DYKE GRAVES

Driving west on State Highway 30 between Decatur and Dayton, the highway passes by the site of Old Washington, once a frontier settlement on the Rhea County side of the Tennessee River. The road also passes by an old home and a historical marker that refers to Judge David Campbell's grave located nearby. The judge lies buried in the Old Washington Cemetery, several hundred yards behind the house.

But the judge is not alone in his crypt. Buried beside him is his son-in-law, Dr. Thomas Van Dyke, another significant yet lesser-known Tennessean. The stories of the two men touch on many incidents in the early history of the state.

Judge David Campbell was born in Augusta County, Virginia, in 1750. He served in the American Revolution as a major in the Continental army and soon after the war moved to Greene County, North Carolina (part of Tennessee in the future), when it was formed in 1783.

Campbell practiced law on the frontier and was a companion of other influential Tennesseans, such as John Sevier and William Blount. Campbell became involved with the formation of the short-lived state of Franklin, but in 1787 he was elected to the North Carolina Assembly and selected as judge of the Washington District Superior Court, serving until 1790. That year, he was appointed territorial judge until Tennessee became a state in 1796. During his term, from 1797 to 1809, Judge Campbell found himself at odds with old friends such as Sevier and Blount, barely surviving two attempts to remove him from the bench.

In 1807, Rhea County was formed from Roane County. Judge Campbell, who had moved to the area a few years earlier, donated land for a county seat, and in 1812 Washington (now known as Old Washington) was established near the head of Spring Creek. At the time, Spring Creek was deep enough to allow riverboats to travel a mile upstream to Washington, making it an important river port.

Judge Campbell did not live to see the settlement grow to its later importance, though. He died and was buried near his home in Washington in 1812.

Dr. Thomas J. Van Dyke was born in Dover, Delaware, in 1777, studied medicine in Baltimore and by 1800 was stationed at Fort Southwest Point, where he served as an army surgeon. It was during this time that he met and courted Penelope Smith Campbell, the daughter of Judge David Campbell; he soon married Ms. Campbell. Judge Campbell certainly had some influence

Two men who factored into the story of early East Tennessee history are buried side by side at Old Washington Cemetery in Rhea County. David Campbell was a frontier lawyer and judge. His son-in-law Thomas Van Dyke was a friend of John Sevier's, an army surgeon during the War of 1812 and father of McMinn County Confederate Thomas Nixon Van Dyke. *Photo by Stephanie Guy.*

on young Dr. Van Dyke and would have introduced him to other prominent Tennesseans, including a fiery young lawyer named Andrew Jackson.

In 1803, Jackson became involved in an argument with former governor John Sevier, which resulted in both men meeting later with the intentions of dueling with pistols out near Kingston. Dr. Van Dyke accompanied Jackson, and when the horses became spooked due to the continued arguing between Sevier and Jackson, Van Dyke drew a pistol on the old governor and threatened to shoot him. Luckily for all involved, tempers abated and everyone left with only pride-related injuries.

In 1806, Dr. Van Dyke owned property and slaves in Kingston, was a justice of the peace and was a trustee at Rittenhouse Academy. He and Penelope had five children: Alexander, who joined the U.S. Navy and was lost at sea; Jefferson; Thomas Nixon, who later became a prominent citizen of Athens; Mary, who married General William Smith; and Elizabeth Rhea, who later moved to Alabama.

About 1810, Dr. Van Dyke moved his family to the frontier settlement of Washington, then the seat of Rhea County, on the west bank of the Tennessee River below Kingston. He again served as an army surgeon in two campaigns against the Indians in 1813–14 and died from sickness in 1814 while in camp at Fort Claiborne, Alabama. His body was brought back to his home and was buried beside his father-in-law at Old Washington Cemetery.

Part VI
Holidays and Traditions

As we draw to a close of another edition of "Hidden History," allow me to take you back into my own memories, back into the stories of my own family and growing up in a rural area of Southeast Tennessee. The steep ridges and dark, creek-fed valleys were places I played as a child and where I listened intently to every story my grandparents told me, never realizing that I would one day share them with others.

George Burger's Christmas

It was a cold Christmas day at the Alec Burger home in 1896, with frost covering the farm along the dirt road that curled through the Burger Branch Valley. That morning, Alec had risen early, went out to feed his cows, hogs and horses and placed a few small presents in the stockings that were hung over the hearth.

Normally, he'd have awakened the children in order for them to help with the chores, but it was Christmas, and so he let them sleep while Nancy prepared breakfast. The Burgers did not consider themselves poor, for they were about as well off as any of their neighbors, and the few presents that filled the four stockings were about the standard amount that any of the children in the area might receive. Most of the people on Burger Branch were farmers, like Alec, with a blacksmith here and there and a store owner down at the end of the valley where the road was that connected Athens and White Cliff. A few presents were better than nothing at all, and some children he knew would not have a thing. But he and Nancy had gathered and sold a few extra eggs in the fall, and the Burger children would have a Christmas this year.

Finally, they woke as the sun rose. George was the youngest, along with his older sisters Sallie, Callie and Mandy. Being the youngest and also the only boy, George was a bit spoiled, and Alec worried a little about the temper and selfishness that the ten-year-old occasionally showed. But Alec himself was part to blame, for he'd bought George a special present this year. He had ridden his horse all the way to Athens to get it, and as the children gathered around the blazing fireplace, he was especially anxious for George to open his gift.

Nancy took each stocking down carefully, handing it to each of the children, still dressed in their nightshirts. They began to draw out their gifts: a few pieces of stick candy, a small doll, an apple and a tasty orange, which the children rarely got to have. Finally, George drew out the gift wrapped in crude brown paper, and Alec watched happily as George fumbled with the string and held up the present.

It was a brown porcelain dog—sitting up on its hind legs, tongue lolled out and about four inches tall. The girls immediately took notice of the statue and, with envious looks, made admiring comments of how beautiful it was and how much their father must have paid for it. But Alec's joy was short-lived.

Perhaps it was being embarrassed by his sisters' praise, or maybe it was just being spoiled that caused him to do it—for George suddenly grew red-faced and leapt to his feet. He grasped the dog in his hands and cried, "This ain't what I wanted!" To Alec's horror, George drew back his hand and threw the porcelain dog into the fireplace.

The sound of glass breaking shattered the Christmas and was immediately mixed with Nancy's voice: "George Burger! What in the world? How could you—"

"It ain't what I wanted! Stupid ole dog!"

"But dad bought that for you!" scolded Mandy.

"I don't care!" screamed the boy as he turned and ran back to the bedroom. The others could barely look at Alec, who sighed and stared out the window at the frozen ground.

It was sometime later, after he'd watched his sisters playing with their own Christmas presents, that the burning regret came to George, and it was compounded by the quiet disappointment he saw in his father's eyes. A day or so later, when it was his chore to clean the ashes from the fireplace, the boy searched the blackened stone corners for his gift. He could find only the dog's head among the ashes.

Years came and went, and George grew to be a man as his father grew old. Eventually, George had his own wife and children and then his own grandchildren. Sometimes, on cold winter days, he would think of his parents lying in their graves at old Liberty Hill, and he would think about his father's gift of the porcelain dog and of a boy's selfish mistake.

Another Christmastime came, and George was an old, widowed man, still living in the same old house with his daughter and son-in-law and his grandchildren, when it was decided to remove the old chimney. Its stones had been placed more than one hundred years before, and George's son-in-law had bought concrete blocks to build a new chimney for a new wood stove. All afternoon, George sat nearby in his chair, watching the work as the stones were slowly taken down through the roof and down to the hearth. Then, one of his grandsons said something that caught his attention.

"Look here at this," said the boy, holding something in his dirty hand. "What is this old thing?"

George stood up, walked to the boy and took the grimy porcelain in his own hand again, smoothing away the dirt from a dog's body.

"Do you know what it is, Grandpa?" asked the curious child.

George went carefully into his room as the children followed and quietly searched through the wardrobe by his bed. In a few minutes, he turned to the children and, with a smile, placed his hands together and rejoined the dog's head with his body. The children gasped. "Grandpa! What is that?"

George wiped his misty eyes and sat down on the bed as the children gathered around him. "Well, you see, this was a gift my dad gave me for Christmas, a very long time ago."

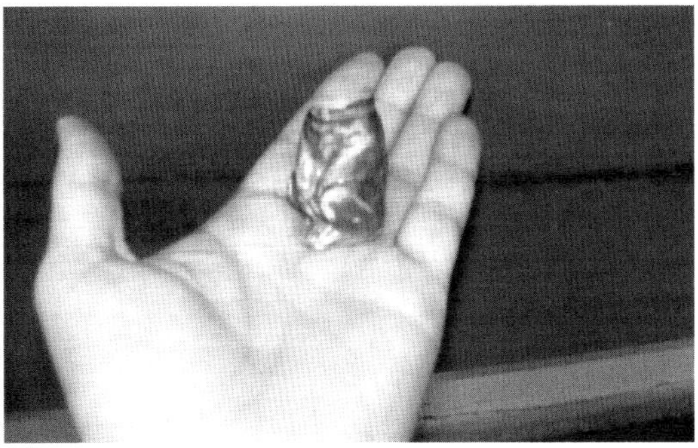

This porcelain dog, found by my mother and her cousins in the ruins of an old chimney in the family home when they were children, connected their aged grandfather to a Christmas story from long ago. The head, unfortunately, has again been lost. *Photo by Stephanie Guy.*

NO FAKE CHRISTMAS TREES, BEAGLES AND MAMAW'S HOUSE

I swore as a child that I would never own a "fake" Christmas tree. Whenever my mother suggested such a heretical act, I immediately flew to the defense of real trees. "It's not the same! It's not Christmasy!" I would say, ready to picket and boycott any attempts to introduce a plastic and wire tree into the house. My parents, being good ones, rolled their eyes and succumbed yearly to the tree demands from me and my brother, even into our college years.

Today, my mother enjoys looking at the twelve-foot artificial tree in my house and reminding me about my former real-tree-only principles. Now I roll my eyes and ramble on about the mess and fire hazards of real trees. Funny what being a parent does to you.

The reason why I once was such a militant child when it came to real Christmas trees was the fact that there were never any artificial trees, and actually few "cultivated" Christmas trees, that were ever brought into my Mamaw and Papaw's house. Like most kids, my grandparents set the standard for any holiday celebrations and family gatherings, so if my grandparents never had a fake tree, to have one would certainly have been sinful.

Again, as there were no "fakes," there were few "store-bought trees" (as my grandfather called them) at their house. So in a somewhat countrified, not-exactly-Norman-Rockwell fashion, this is how we got Mamaw's Christmas tree. I dare say this was how it was once done by many people in Southeast Tennessee.

First of all, there was none of this "putting up a tree the day after Thanksgiving" business (which now I am as guilty of as anybody). No tree would pass over Mamaw's threshold until at least the second week in December. This had nothing to do with the purity of the season. It was a practical matter: a real tree would dry out if brought inside too soon, and Papaw's wood heater would only accelerate this effect.

So, about that second week of December, my aunts would call everybody, and with the whole family living in the same valley, we would soon assemble at Mamaw's. She would, by then, have a corner cleared out in the living room, which normally consisted of relocating a small black-and-white television to another corner so that it was still readily visible from Papaw's recliner—which, it is important to note, was never, ever moved. My mother and her sisters would occupy the living room and, at times, assist Mamaw in cooking supper, while the five grandkids loaded up in the back of a pickup truck along with an axe, some rope, a flashlight and no more than two beagles. Papaw and at least one uncle rode in the cab. It would always be cold and dark, and the wind would whip through us like knives as we jumbled along the road. We took turns holding the beagles because they were warm and distracted us from the winter air.

Since we lived in the country, there were plenty of places to get a tree. Papaw would drive for a few minutes, stop and peer out his window and then drive a little more and do the same. This went on for perhaps an hour: going and stopping, going and stopping, as he and an uncle tried to find the one tree that, one, was just the right height for Mamaw's living room, and two, was "full," as Papaw called it. Although every tree we looked at seemed to be the same to us, we were convinced that he knew something we didn't. We weren't looking for pines, and since spruces didn't grow around here, our selection was limited to the same tree every year: the cedar.

When he finally stopped, we waited in the truck bed for Papaw and our uncle to cut the tree; it was yet another narrow, scrubby, prickly, aromatic cedar that they placed in the bed of the truck with us, same as the year before and the year before that. It never seemed to be an issue that we were cutting a tree out from someone else's property, and no one ever complained about it. Once done, we held on tight to the beagles and headed back to Mamaw's.

The tree was measured and the excess trunk cut off so that the top would barely miss the ceiling, and once my dad and uncles had screwed on the one-hundred-year-old metal tree stand, it was brought in and placed in the corner. For a few seconds we would admire it, the Christmas spirit now officially stirring in our hearts, and then it would fall over. Dad and an uncle or two would wrestle with it, while Papaw muttered something about how if the trunk had been cut off straight in the first place like he'd told them it would sit right in the metal stand. Finally, the tree decided to stand still, and everybody agreed that it was as good of a tree as last year's. Mamaw brought out the box of ornaments. We decorated it, stuffing into the thick greenery glass balls, plastic Santas, strings of gold or silver garland and multicolored string lights with little clear bulb holders that looked like flowers. When it was all done, the entire tree was then covered in tin icicle garland, which was literally thrown onto the tree by an aunt who said that she was the only one who knew how to do it without making a mess.

The grandkids repeatedly asked when presents were going to be put under the tree. Then we would eat supper as the lights blinked, and as the evening passed we sat around to hear tales of Santa Claus and stories from the adults of their own Chrismases from long ago. Those stories from so many years before were always my favorite part. This was how every Christmas started—at least that's the way I remember it, from so many years now distant.

My artificial tree is beautiful, and on it are some of those same ornaments that once decorated Mamaw's trees. In order for me to defend myself against my mother's reminders, my wife and I still decorate with a few live evergreen boughs so that there is at least a touch of tradition still in our family. When we cut the evergreen boughs, there is always one particular species that tends to be used more than the others.

To this day, I still have a thing for cedar.

CAT HEADS FOR BREAKFAST

I grew up in the rural Burger Branch community on the McMinn-Monroe County line, which consists of hillside farms stretching along a shallow valley and creek that bears the name of my Burger ancestors, who first settled there about 1830. Growing up, we were not poor, but no one along Burger Branch was ever considered rich, either. There was no cable television out there, and there still isn't; there were also no city waterlines—only wells and springs. We were fortunate to have electricity and phones, although we had party lines. These were not the "party lines" advertised today but rather were phone lines shared by two or more neighbors so that everyone knew everyone else's business. As a young boy, I used my grandparents' outside toilet, a two-seater that my grandfather and uncle had built. Actually, I never figured out the use for that other seat, as no one ever "shared the experience," to my knowledge. I think he built it that way to make the neighbors a little envious.

My brother and I often had friends from school spend the night with us. It was a real treat for our friends who lived in town or in subdivisions to come and enjoy the seemingly endless space on our family's small farm and experience a little rural life among the porch dogs, barn cats, chickens, goats, cattle, horses and occasional pig. Our friends sometimes called our economic situation into question after we went to church on Sunday, as we worshiped at the Church of Christ at Liberty Hill. The Church of Christ is very literal when it comes to the Bible, and since the Bible says to "sing and make melody in your heart," that is exactly what we did—pure congregational singing with no instruments. Our denominational friends often pitied us when they saw everyone singing without instrumental music and asked if we were just too poor to buy a piano.

My grandparents, Kenneth and Inez Morgan, had been teenagers in the Great Depression, and the experience of making do never left them. "Papaw" never got rid of anything. He would use the sides of old leather boots for barn door hinges and never owned a tractor—choosing to own horses he could either ride or use to plow his gardens. "Mamaw" had the softest hands I ever saw, which is remarkable considering that she worked either in the house or on the farm every day of her life. She would make her own breakfast syrup by boiling down sugar mixed with water and then pour the thick, hot "sugar syrup" over the bread she made.

Her biscuit bread was always homemade—never from a can. If one of us had brought in a can of biscuits, she'd have made sure that we were on the front pew of church publicly declaring our sin the very next Sunday. She hand-kneaded her dough and prepared it one of two ways: either as a single pan of flatbread that she referred to as "Johnny Cake," or she cut out biscuits with a glass tumbler that, when baked, rose up thick and steamy, "big as a cat's head" she would say.

I remember once when my brother's friend Josh came to spend a weekend with us. We woke up early on Saturday, ate breakfast at Mamaw's and spent the rest of the day with my cousins wading creeks, building forts and chasing chickens. Every now and then, one of us would wander back to Mamaw's kitchen for a quick snack, which is where Josh wound up that afternoon. A few minutes later, we saw him burst out the door and sprint for the woods. We finally found him, high in the top of a cedar tree.

"I ain't never comin' back here again" is all he would say. We finally coaxed him down, and he stood there, wild-eyed and covered in cedar sap, as he told us what had spooked him.

"Your Mamaw…that woman," he stuttered, "she asked me to do something terrible." We asked him what on earth he was talking about, and in a shaking voice he replied, "I was in the kitchen and she said, 'Josh, you want something to eat?' and I said, 'Yes'm,' and she said, 'Well I got something for you right here on the stove. I'm gonna let you eat this big cat head.'"

"Well, I tell you right now…I didn't stick around to see which cat it was from."

About the Author

Joe Guy is a syndicated newspaper columnist, the author of several books on law enforcement and regional history and a storyteller and conference speaker. Since 2010, he has served as sheriff in McMinn County, Tennessee, where he is also the county historian. He resides on a small farm located near Englewood with his wife and sons.